DON'T BE A MULE

A DOWN-TO-EARTH, COMMON-SENSE
APPROACH TO SAVING MORE, SPENDING
LESS, AND GENERATING EXTRA MONEY IN
YOUR EVERYDAY LIFE.

DAVID BAKKE

ISBN: 1-4392-5916-X
ISBN-13: 9781439259160

Visit www.booksurge.com to order additional copies.

Dedication

To Mary and Russ, for everything…

TABLE OF CONTENTS

FOREWARD

I wanted to spend just a few short minutes discussing the idea behind the title of this book. As you will see, I do not refer back to it very often throughout the book. I had come up with several other working titles for the book before I decided on this particular one.

The reason that I decided on this title for the book is because I felt that it is the overall piece of advice that I am trying to impart to you, the reader. It basically means what it says: "Don't Be a Mule."

Some quick examples—

When you are doing your grocery shopping—Don't Be a Mule. Don't mindlessly wander through the aisles picking up the same overpriced items that you always do when you could take off the blinders, open your eyes, and start saving yourself some money (see chapter 3).

When you are paying your bills—Don't Be a Mule. Do not robotically open up the envelopes, look at the amounts due, write out your checks, lick the stamps, and send them off. Check your utility bills for accuracy, really *really* check your credit card bills for mistakes, and if you find something wrong with any of them, then REALLY don't be a mule; stand up and fight for the money that's rightfully yours (see Chapter 4).

When you get home from work at night—Don't Be A Mule. Instead of sitting down in front of the TV for a mindless three hours of boob-tube watching, actually think about what you are passionate about and what you can provide value to in someone else's life. This is the key and the beginning to being able to generate extra cash, without even getting a second job (see Chapter 5).

And there you have it, an explanation of what the title really means....

INTRODUCTION

The Basics of Saving in Your Everyday Life

The purpose of this book is to help you improve the condition of what I like to call your "personal economy." I feel that this book can be helpful to people in all types of financial situations. Are you knee-deep in credit card debt? I think I can help. Are you just trying to save some money in your everyday life? This book can definitely get you on the right track. Are your finances in pretty good shape, but you just want to find a way to generate some income in your life without getting a second job? I have you covered there as well. But before we go any further I do want to let you know that none of this should be construed as professional, binding financial advice. It is just a great deal of things that worked for me and that I am quite confident can work for you.

I wanted to make this book a tool for people in all types of financial situations and for people in all walks of life. I can assure you that I am just a regular guy—I never studied finance,

I have never worked for a financial services company, and I have never been rich. I think that all of these facts give me the basis for being able to help people who are similar to me. The reason I say that is when I was looking for help with my financial situation, I did try speaking to people who studied finance. Do you know what they told me?? A bunch of "book" answers that never really made any sense and did not seem to be based in the real world. And when I made the huge mistake of talking to people in the financial services world, do you know what I got? All kinds of people who wanted nothing more than to sell me some sort of financial product that was going to "fix" all of my problems. In this book, you will see some breaks in my writing where I will stop to give you one of many financial "alerts." Here is the first one:

ALERT:

You can solve all of your financial worries and make the most of your financial opportunities without spending a dime on ANY kind of financial product. This goes for anything ranging from some financial software to help you track your finances, to what I call the worst of all—debt consolidation companies. NEVER even consider using one of them.

Now, of course, I am sure that your first response to this is, "Well, aren't you asking me to spend money to buy this book?" Well, yes, I am. But I will also tell you this: I fought hard to keep the price of this book low, because my main motivation in writing this is not to make money, but to help people. Additionally, I feel the information in this book would cost a fortune if purchased separately, and also, the degree to which you can improve your financial situation by purchasing this book far outweighs its small cost.

But back to my point. There was a part about that whole thing that I never really understood. If I am trying to save money, or even to spend less money, why would I purchase some expensive financial product or service to do it? I quickly dismissed those people. I decided a long time ago that if I was smart enough to get myself into the financial mess that I was in, then I was smart enough to get myself out of it without spending any additional money.

Of course, that's not to say that I figured all of this out on my own, not at all. I had plenty of help along the way. I even have a section in this book that explains that as well—the people you need to have in your circle of contacts that can help you. And finally, at one point, I thought to myself, well, maybe I need to talk to some rich people about my problems. After all, they're rich, right? Well, either I had some bad luck in whom I chose to speak to, or the rich people I did talk to either never had the problems that I was having, or they forgot about what it was like to have those problems way back whenever.

What I am trying to do is to create a place where people can go for concrete, usable, relevant advice on how to, among other things, save more money in their everyday lives. This also includes how to spend less money on the things that we do buy, and ways to generate income in your daily life without having to go out and get a second job. I will get to a little more about myself here in a minute, but to go through my so-called "financial timeline," I begin with a brief summary. Of course, if you are not interested, feel free to skip this part and move on to the nuts and bolts part of this book. However, I do think there is some relevance to my story, so you may want to spend a few minutes reading it. The choice is yours.

From there, I go into the mental aspects of what I did to improve my financial situation. The most important thing I learned (unfortunately, this was done in hindsight), is that this whole escape that I made from the depths of financial hell had a lot more to do with my mindsets and thoughts about money rather than the actual concrete things that I changed in my life. It is much more important to change your attitudes towards money, and how you view its importance, than the actual steps you take in your life. I say this because without the first, the second will never happen. Or at least, it will never happen long enough in your life to make a difference.

After this, the book is broken down into two more sections—ways to *save more money* in your life and ways to *spend less money*.

And finally, I include a section at the end of this book that I think takes the whole journey full circle, and that is the section about generating more income for YOU. After I spent so long in setting up my systems to save money and everything that I do to spend less money, I actually found myself with a fair amount of free time on my hands. And by this point in my life, I was of course interested in making more money for myself. What I was not interested in was changing careers or trying to find a new job to do it. What I began to do was try to find ways to generate income for myself basically in my spare time. I think this whole concept is something that would appeal to a great many people. Additionally, it is also the way that many entrepreneurs and small business owners get started. What began as something that they did in their spare time became such a success for them that it became their main source of income and allowed them to work for themselves, so to speak. I do not profess to be at that point yet, and it is not necessarily a direct goal of mine at this time, but who knows, if writing this book proves to be successful maybe the same thing will happen to me.

And then there is a closing section with some final thoughts. So, read this from cover to cover if you choose, or browse though and find the stuff that only applies to you. I'd like to think of it as something that is close to a "one-stop shop" for most of the ways to improve your finances, and I think there is something in it for everyone. One thing that I can claim so far is that I have yet to meet someone to whom I was unable to offer some way to save money, spend less money, or make money in their spare time. I have always been able to find something.

There is one final thought that I'd like to include before we get started. This book IS a lot of things, and it is also NOT a lot of things. What it *is* should be pretty obvious once you've read the first several pages. I think it is a combination of both a mental strategy and a concrete strategy on what you need to do to improve your finances, get out of debt, or start to simply save more of your money (with the emphasis being on the mental aspect).

One thing this book is NOT is an all–inclusive guide on how you can improve your water bill, or every single way ever come up with on how to impact your electric bill. I do list a lot of ways to impact these things, but for the comprehensive list, consult the Internet. Like I said, this book is more about developing the long-term habits you'll need for lasting financial liberty than it is about your power bill.

During the many revisions of this book, I was continually approached by anyone and everyone who came to me and said, "Hey, you forgot to include this way how to improve your gas bill," or "Don't forget to put in how if you do such and such, your power bill will go down." Like I said, that is one thing this book is not. I have included several relevant ways to impact all of these bills, but certainly not an all-inclusive list. I think it is even more important to learn and take on the mental steps needed to put all of these changes into place. You can have a list of the hundred best ways to lower your water bill, but if you don't know how to put them into place and how to make them habits, then you're just wasting time....

So enjoy the read; I think you'll like it!

CHAPTER I

The Beginning of the End

"My problem lies in reconciling my gross habits with my net income." -
Errol Flynn

Late '80s to early '90s—fun fun fun!

I think it all began one day when I was walking across the campus of the college that I was attending at the time. They had a little table set up somewhere and they were signing up college students for credit cards. The "pitch" was that college students were recently deemed to be good "credit risks" and they were offering some deal on a credit card. At the time, I never had a credit card before (and I think my parents may have had one or two in their lifetime). But goodness, was it a great concept. I could actually purchase things without paying for them—I just had to give them some little piece of plastic and I could take my things home. Wow, I thought. I signed on the bottom line as fast as I could. I think I probably bought two or three things on the way home from school that day.

As it turns out, it wasn't that college students were deemed to be good "credit risks" at all. It was actually that the credit card companies figured out that college students were a great demographic niche for them to MAKE MONEY. It was true then, and I am sure that it still is today.

And guess what? With me, it worked! It wasn't like I was out of control or anything. But I completely ignored the fact that I would actually have to pay for all the things that I had bought at some point in time. I think my limit on that first card was $500 and I probably reached that in the first few months. Of course the credit card company gladly obliged me and raised my limit. Before long, I had signed up for a few more cards and before you knew it, I was on a roll!

One of the worst things about this whole beginning is that I couldn't even tell you what I spent all that money on. It wasn't like it was for some major purchase of some item that I wanted. It was just so easy (it seemed) at the time to just spend money whenever I wanted. I went out to eat all the time, I went out with my friends a lot more—it was just lots of little things. Well, after a few years, I was pretty far into debt with my many different credit cards. It was all I could do to pay the minimums, and a lot of the time, even that did not happen.

Early to mid-90s—the wake-up call

I think I finally began to "wake up" financially sometime in the mid-90s. I remember one morning walking out to the kitchen in my parents' house where I was staying at the time because I was "in between" jobs, and there was a note on the kitchen table.

It was from my parents, and I'll never forget it. It basically said:

"David. This is your current financial situation, as much as we know about it. You owe us about $10K from the money you have borrowed from us over the past year [*because of my unsteady job situation*]. You made $14K last year, and were unable to pay us back anything. Your credit card debt is approximately $15K.

"We are writing you this message because we love you. At this rate, you will first of all, never be able to pay us back the money you owe us, and although we love you, we do expect that you pay it back. Second, you will be in debt to credit card companies for the rest of your life.

"We are proposing taking over your finances for a period of time to be determined by how fast we can get your bills paid off. We will still make sure you have money to live, but probably not to live the way you have been living the past year or so. Please let us know. Love, Mom & Dad."

Well, if this wasn't a wake-up call for me, I don't know what was. I have no idea how they got their hands on my financial situation, but that was the least of my worries. First, I had no idea I owed them so much money, and second, I had never taken the time to look at it from the big picture as to how much I really owed the credit card companies.

And finally, the thought of someone having to take over my finances for me, and to actually be put back on an allowance (something I hadn't been on since I was what, seven years old?), embarrassed the hell out of me.

It was then and there that I decided to do something about it.

I moved out shortly thereafter (not because of the note but because I had actually found a decent paying job) and it was then that I completely re-thought my ideas about money, about managing it, and about how I wanted to live my life.

Let me also tell you about the two instances that will stick with me forever—and the main reason why I want to help people. They both happened when I was in the process of transforming my thoughts about money and credit cards and so on. I was in my late twenties, and was about as broke as broke could be. I was working in a restaurant as a kitchen manager. The uniform for that particular job was a chef's coat that the company gave me, black jeans, and black tennis shoes. Pretty simple, right? Well, my boss was kind of a stickler about uniforms, and I wasn't, but he was always checking me out to make sure my uniform looked good. Well, after about two weeks of him staring down at the tennis shoes I had on, I finally asked him if everything was OK. He pulled me aside, and said, "Dave, I'm not trying to embarrass you, but have you ever REALLY looked at those shoes you have on?" Well, the answer to that question was no (I had a lot of denial issues back then, as you'll soon see). When we both looked at them, it was extremely embarrassing. They were the nastiest, smelliest, stinkiest shoes you could ever imagine. About two or three holes in each one and you could almost smell those things coming! I never realized it because at that point in time, if I didn't have money for something I needed, I just tried to ignore it. I had to break down and tell my boss the real reason for my nasty shoes. We were actually pretty good friends, so it wasn't that bad, but it was still embarrassing. I actually had to tell my boss that the reason for me wearing those shoes to work was that *I couldn't afford new ones.*

So my boss had to give me money (I think he felt too sorry for me to ask me to pay it back) just to buy a decent pair of shoes to go to work in.

The second little story occurred about a year after the shoe incident. My boss and I had become quite successful at the restaurant we opened. The place was happenin'—sales were up, customer counts were up, the parking lot was full almost every night. I had asked my boss for a weekend off and he gave it to me because he said I deserved it. I didn't really have anything planned, I just wanted the weekend off. I wasn't going out of town or anything (surprise, surprise—I couldn't afford to go anywhere even if I wanted to).

At the last minute, my boss told me that the big bosses had planned a last-minute trip to our restaurant for that weekend I wanted off. I asked him if he wanted me to work instead of being off. He told me no, but he did say that he wasn't sure why they were coming—and they might want to talk to me, so I needed to stay close to my phone. OK, no big deal. I spent my weekend doing not much of anything, but no one from work ever called me. I didn't think anything of it until I returned to work the following Monday.

My boss pulled me aside and asked me what was going on. I told him nothing, I had just enjoyed my weekend. It was then that he proceeded to tell me that the big bosses had come to town, and they wanted to discuss promotions with the both of us. "Why didn't you call me then?" I asked. It was then that he told me that they had tried to call a few times but got the recorded message that my phone was disconnected. Yup, *my phone was disconnected.* First, I completely forgot about paying the bill, even though I doubt I could have afforded it at the time anyways. Second, obviously, the big bosses couldn't get in touch with me, so they couldn't discuss a promotion with me, and also questioned whether I even wanted it since I couldn't even be reached (by the way, I think cell phones were out by then, but of course I couldn't afford one). This part wasn't a big deal, but what frustrated me the most was the thoughts that were probably in the back of the minds of these big bosses. And these thoughts were spoken to my boss. They told him, "Do we really want to give this guy more responsibility if he can't even keep his telephone turned on?" I am sure you all know how big bosses are—they have been known to blow things out of proportion—but in a sense, they were right. For at least the next year, whenever they came to town, they would always ask my boss if I had gotten my act together yet, was I responsible enough for a promotion, and so on.

These two embarrassments finally motivated me to do something serious about my finances, and these two stories are still with me. It is what motivates me to this day to continue to find ways to decrease my bills, save more of the money I have, and to increase the money I have coming in.

By the way, I eventually got my promotion, but can you imagine how much more quickly I could have dug myself out of the financial hole I was in had I just paid my phone bill on time?

Now, I want to be clear on something—I know I mentioned some things earlier about being "in-between" jobs and about finding one and so forth, but I want to tell you that my ability to turn my financial life around had very little to do with going from not having any income to having some high-paying job. Of course, I did have some pay increases over the years which made this process a little faster, but the main reason I was able to do it was because I changed my mental approach towards money and finances.

Don't get me wrong, there were some sacrifices made along the way, but as I look back on it now, there are no times I can remember now of missing out on "this" or not being able to do "that." The major reason for me accomplishing what I did financially was because I put my mind to it that I would get out of debt and never go back in debt again, and that I was WILLING to do what it took in the short term to see this happen.

Mid-to-late '90s—the tip of the iceberg

At this point in time, after I put my mind to it that I would get out of this mess I'd put myself into, I can tell you that I had no systems in place and I had not even thought out a lot of the concepts that I will outline in this book; I was simply "doing." Which would be a good start for any of you reading this book right now, depending on the situation you're in. If your situation seems too big and broad and deep, so to speak, and you think you'll never be able to get out of it no matter what you do (which is exactly how I thought plenty of times), then you just need to start doing SOMETHING.

Basically, the first thing that I did was cut up the credit cards that I had left which I could still charge on. Most of them were over their limits and had been closed by the credit card companies themselves. I wasn't even allowed to have a bank account for several years because of the amount of checks that I had bounced.

On a side note, when I began to get serious about this, I looked at my records and I made $26,000 that first year. So again, it certainly did not have that much to do with the money I was making; it had to do with how I was spending the money that I made.

I decided to start doing several things, and again, in no particular order.

1. Double the minimums

First off, this book is not strictly about getting out of credit card debt. I mean, I am sure that this is an important aspect to address for anyone who is trying to impact their finances, but there is not really much concrete advice that I can give to you other than to simply pay them off. Of course, if you decide to utilize some of the mindset changes that I go over in this book, your credit card debt will take care of itself. It will only be a matter of time. And the amount of time that it takes will simply depend on how deep in the hole you are and how disciplined you are.

I decided that I would "double" the minimum monthly payment on any and all credit cards. This is another key that I will address in my credit card debt section. If you look at what the minimum monthly payment is on your credit card statements, and that is all you are paying on them, you will basically be in debt to them for the rest of your life. Which is exactly what the credit card company wants.

There are all kinds of examples that you can find that say it will take you so many years to pay this off by paying the minimums, and so on; suffice to say, for posterity's sake, if you only pay the minimum you'll be in debt with these people for the REST OF YOUR LIFE. Not particularly accurate, but this mindset worked for me.

2. Open checking account

Now, for most of you, I would assume that you have a checking account, and have always had one. So I know this step is probably already taken care of. Honestly, I am really only including this to clarify to you how bad off I really was.

One of my restaurant jobs required me to transfer to Birmingham, Alabama. This occurred I think in 1993. After getting settled, one of the things I had to do was to go open my checking account. You have no idea how embarrassing it was to be told by the bank employee that basically I had bounced so many checks and had overdrawn my account so many times, that I was actually ineligible for a checking account! This was another reality check for me that woke me up also. Goodness, I didn't even know that one could be ineligible for a checking account, but guess what, I was! I asked them what I could do in the meantime and he told me that the only thing I could do was to wait, and to pay my bills on time. I was finally able to open a checking account sometime around 1998.

Without belaboring the point, do you have any idea what this meant for me? Basically, it meant FIVE YEARS of going to gas stations and post offices and wherever else they sold money orders every single month to pay my bills. It meant never being able to write a check for anything (obviously), and of course, I had no credit cards at the time either. They had all been closed by the credit card companies long before.

I could do nothing but carry cash on me wherever I went. So, in addition to everything else, it was five years of a safety risk as well. Thank God, though, nothing ever happened to me.

I will never forget the day I walked out of that bank with my first checking account in five years. This was another one of those "I vow I'll never go back" moments. Meaning, it was at that point that I vowed to myself that I would never let myself get into that financial mess again, no matter what it took. I would never let myself suffer the embarrassment of being denied a checking account again, and I would never go through the hassle, and the waste of time and money of buying money orders every month to pay my bills.

In addition to those things, I started to institute basically everything that I talk about in the next 150 pages into my life. Looking back on it, the majority of it was changing my mindset on money and how I viewed it as it came into my life and how it went out of my life. Once I was able to get my "financial" head on straight, everything else seemed to simply drop right into order. Or at least, the concrete steps that I took in my life were much easier to implement once I was in the right frame of mind. And all of these mental aspects and learned habits will be outlined in detail in the next chapter.

Late '90s—breathing room

After instituting all of that in my personal life, after about a few years, I finally began to see some concrete, actual results. It was amazing. It was an unbelievable feeling to not have to be thinking about how to pay bills before utilities were shut off, it was an amazing feeling to actually have money in my wallet, and there were a bunch of other amazing feelings all over the place.

Of course, I was not completely out of the soup yet. The two biggest "debts" that I had at this point in my life were to my credit cards and to my parents. It was just not feasible to try to pay back one and then the other, so I had to begin both at the same time. (I guess I could have put off my parents, but I had already done that for long enough so I decided to do both at the same time.) By this time, I was well on my way to being completely paid off with my credit cards, and I had at least BEGUN to pay my parents back.

Now, before I get too far into this whole thing, I want to make sure that I am being completely honest with you. I do want to say that this whole endeavor was not an easy process. Of course, getting into debt was **LOTS** of fun. However, the rest of it did involve some hard work and, although not necessarily a lot of sacrifice, a good bit of willpower. But by this time, I was starting to see the light at the end of the tunnel. I was still working at a restaurant—a restaurant which, as a matter of fact, I opened from day one. Not anything that I invested my own money in, but at the time I was employed by a corporate restaurant chain that was expanding, had opened a location near where I lived, and chose me to be one of the store opening managers. Let me tell you, that was a lot of hard work. Much more work than anything I had ever invested in getting myself out of debt. When we first opened up, business was quite slow, and the only way that we were able to build a successful business there was by pounding the pavement to tell people we were there, and working a ton of hours to make sure that the food and service were as close to perfect as close to one hundred percent of the time as possible. Why am I telling you all of this? Because all of that hard work at my job finally began to pay off with some pretty decent-sized bonus checks. All of my ability to get out of my financial difficulties was not completely based on simply managing the money that I was able to make; some of it came from doing what I could professionally to make as much money as I could. Which is also another section in this book and a fairly important part of the quest to solidify my personal economy.

But I digress. So, where did all of that bonus money go? Like I said, I had finally started seeing some extra money at the end of the month after my bills were paid from my new "smart living" that I had begun, so I had about $1,000 extra at the end of each month.

I began to send huge chunks of money to my parents. Up until then, I had really only been sending maybe one to two hundred dollars whenever I could (which was really not that much considering that I owed them close to $10,000).

After I began to send them that kind of money, of course, my mother was all over me telling me that I had to get on a schedule and let's sit down and figure out exactly how much I owed them and let's send a fixed amount every month, etc.

Let me tell you how I handled that. First, I was scared to death to find out exactly how much I owed them because I figured that it would demoralize me, or somehow slow down the momentum that I was building. I did not want to get TOO depressed at the beginning, or too excited along the way. Second, I did not want to start sending them a fixed amount every month. Because if we decided on a set amount and in some particular month I could have sent more, then it would just take me longer to pay them off. I did not want anything to get in my way. I told them, I don't want to know how much I owe you, I am going to send you as much as I can every month till it's paid off, and just call me when I am finished. So I guess you could say I was putting the blinders "on" rather than taking them off.

Well, for whatever reason, it worked. I sent them at least $1,000 a month for right around ten months. I never called and asked for updates, never asked when I was close to being finished, I just kept sending it. Then one day some time after the tenth month, I got a letter in the mail from my parents. They rarely sent me letters, so I was a little surprised.

In it was a simple note: "We don't really know how you got yourself into that money mess, and we really don't know how you got yourself out so fast, but you did it. You're finished. And you even have a little left over." And in with that short note was a check for somewhere around $400. This was another one of those "tear in the eyes" moments. It was also one of those "this thing might finally have an ending to it" kind of moments. I could not believe that I had done it. Paid off my parents? A debt I had owed to them for what, almost eight years? This was another 800-pound gorilla off of my back, and it gave me the further motivation to never ever look back, to never get into that kind of mess again, and to start to make my money work for me, instead of the other way around. Oh, one other thing—I sent them an even shorter note back, replying, "In regards to your not knowing how I got myself into or out of that money mess, I just have three words for you—

Neither do I."

Early to mid-2000—next tip of the iceberg

There was really only one big milestone in my financial journey during this period and that was the purchase of my first home. I had been told by just about everyone that real estate was one of the best investments that one could ever make, and although I may be doubting them these days, I think that in the long run they were all correct. If you compare the situations of renting an apartment versus owning your own home, the differences are easy to see. And this is only speaking from a financial standpoint. Of course, there are also all of the regular benefits to living in a home that I began to enjoy. A lot more privacy, more feeling of being in control, your own yard (wow!), and living in an actual neighborhood. However, financially speaking, when you are renting an apartment, you are virtually giving your money to someone else. You are getting something for that money but that money is no longer yours. With a home, it is actually "investing" your money. That money is *yours*. And when you sell your home, the best thing is, you get it all back, and most of the time, you get back even more!

Shortly after I began my efforts to repay my debts, I began to hear several people around me, namely my close friends and family, that I needed to look into buying a house. Buying a house was far too intimidating of a subject to even begin to think about, but the fact that the people around me were beginning to tell me this sort of thing told me a few things deep down inside—

I must be doing something right.

I must be on the right track.

And finally, if I kept doing what I was doing, someday I might actually be able to get out of my apartment and into my own home.

In 2000, I took the plunge and bought my first home. It was quite an intimidating course of action in the beginning. I didn't know how much higher my bills would be, I did actually feel a little more pressure about my bills, and also, if something went wrong with the house, I certainly didn't have a rental office to call anymore!

But it all worked out in the end. I was so concerned about my bills in the beginning that for a while I had contemplated picking up a second job, but that day never came. I continued to pay my bills on time, every time, and never looked back. The amounts that my bills went up were minimal, really, and the benefits of owning a home from a financial standpoint were great—but what was even better were the benefits that I enjoyed on a daily basis. As I said, much more peace and quiet, parking in my own driveway at night and all of the other little things that go along with home ownership. On a side note, the thing about not being able to call the rental office if something went wrong in my home turned out to really be a good thing, because I have very much enjoyed becoming a "do-it-yourself-er" around my house!

Now, I want to spend a little time here talking about what I did after my major debts were finally paid off. Not too much time, just a little. The reason being is that this book is much more about how to get yourself to this point rather than what to start doing once you get there. The point is that after you get to the place where I got (i.e., completely out of debt), that is not the time to stop working on your personal economy. Actually, that's where the fun begins. That's the point where you get your money working for you, instead of the other way around.

I had just purchased my first home, and had purchased all of the little things that go along with moving into your new home. These "little things" for me added up to about $3,000. Of course, it was before I had a personal computer at home and before I really knew anything about the Internet, so I am sure had I really been on my savings "game" that I could have about cut that number in half. But what's done is done. That's another thing I learned along the way. Whenever I come up with a new way to save money or a less expensive way to buy something that I buy a lot of, I always find myself kind of kicking myself in the rear for not thinking of it sooner. I have since learned to quash this feeling because it is simply counterproductive. You cannot keep doing that to yourself along the way or it will kill your enthusiasm and motivation. The only constructive way that you can look at it is as feedback and a learning experience and just be happy that you found another way to save.

So I was finally in my new home, I had paid my bills on time for the first few months (the utilities did not even really go up that much—it wasn't that big of a townhome) and about a year or so later, I found myself with approximately $10,000 in the bank. Actually, it was probably close to two years. I don't want you to think there was some magic going on. I just want to further emphasize that once you get going on this program and begin to eliminate all of the debt and waste in your life, your disposable income will rise at a rate much faster than you would have ever expected. Actually, let me repeat myself and make an alert out of that:

ALERT:

Once you get going on this program and begin to eliminate all of the debt and waste in your life, your disposable income will rise at a rate much faster than you would have ever expected.

I did receive a decent raise or two at work, but I will not use that as an excuse or make it sound like that's the only reason I finally had extra money. I got a few good raises at work because it was *part of my whole plan*. You will read more about that later.

So, what to do with this extra money? To be honest with you, it just sat in a zero-percent-earning savings account for about six months. Can you imagine? It just sat there, doing nothing for me. Well, that is where having the right people in your circle of contacts comes in to play. You will learn later on in Chapter 8 that one of those people is a good finance person. Meaning, someone you can trust who knows a lot about money matters. Maybe it is a financial planner, maybe a relative who is good with their money, goodness, maybe it will even end up being me for some of you out there. I hope so.

As you will also learn in Chapter 8, that person for me was and is my mother. She worked in the insurance industry for approximately twenty-five years, and spent her retirement studying money matters. Yup, that's the extent of her money knowledge, but do you know what? You can learn a ton about money by just reading, and I trust that woman's advice more than anybody in this world. And a lot of the reasons why are the same reasons that I think that you should listen to me. She is a "real-world" type of person who is not out to sell me anything, who is not insanely rich, and who understands the day-to-day issues that confront most of us financially.

She had always told me that after you get to the point that I did, you should have six months worth of expenses set aside just in case. The "just in case" part means just in case you lose your job unexpectedly, just in case you die and you have a wife and kids to take care of, etc. These will probably never happen, but it is a good idea. However, if you are able to get yourself into this position (actually, if you can at least come up with three months expenses, I think you'd be doing great), what you should also realize is that this money does not have to have this as its sole purpose. What I mean by that is that you don't need to put it somewhere where it is not working for you because it is serving as your emergency fund.

I basically had my emergency expense money set aside, and that's when my mother and I spoke about what to do with the rest. She and I were both pretty shocked that I was able to amass that kind of little nest egg in such a short time after being hopelessly in debt, but she told me that I needed to start getting my money to "work for me" instead of the other way around. The sacrificing part was basically over for me, the working 'hard" on my finances was basically over. Now, I wanted to work "smarter" with my money and get it to work harder for me than I did for it.

To explain this more simply, this means that when you get yourself to the point where you have extra income that you don't need on a monthly basis, you can place this money in a variety of things that will actually generate more income for you without you really doing anything.

I had no idea where these places were, but again, that is where your circle of contacts comes in, and again, for me that was my mother. You'll learn more about what I did with my extra money and some good options for you to do the same in Chapter 5.

I will close this section with one other brief story. After these seven or eight years of hard work, of thought process adjustments, of changing my lifestyle, and of my sacrifices, I finally decided that after all of this, that I really would reward myself. Now, this *entire* story will probably be some other book for me at a much later point in time, but basically, I rewarded myself with a vacation trip overseas to Moscow, Russia, and this is where I met my present wife. It was a trip of amazing experiences and sights and of course memories, and these will remain with me for the rest of my life.

However, this is not the point of the book so there is no reason to go into the details of the trip, but it was quite an amazing experience and worth every penny to me.

Now, before I move on to the next and most recent section of my financial journey, I want to give you some more motivation. I know for me, one of the bigger motivating factors in staying on this path was the major stress that was lifted off of my shoulders when I no longer had to worry about how I was going to pay my bills every single month. The whole endless cycle of continually calling utility companies and begging for more time, watching interest/late charges pile up on my credit cards, robbing Peter to pay Paul, so to speak, all of these things do take a toll on your mind and probably your body. I don't remember exactly at what point it took place, but when all of this went away, it was an unbelievable feeling. Such a great feeling that I told myself that I would never, ever return to living my life in that fashion again.

Well, here comes another one of those feelings. Of course, when you join a 401K, your money is making money for you, but it is a little difficult to see this. You will get a quarterly statement to tell you how your investments are doing, and nine times out of ten they do make money, but it is difficult to really enjoy these gains because again it's a little difficult to read, and also, this is money for your retirement. So, it's not like you could go out and enjoy it if you really wanted to. Now, a money market account is a different story (I will discuss exactly what these are and what they do in Chapter 5). This is another one of those unbelievable feelings. When I opened my first money market, I think I had put somewhere around $4,000 in it. And after that first month, I checked my statement, and I think I had generated $40 in one month. Well, that was an incredible feeling to me. Yes, it was only $40, but you know what? After one year, I checked it and I made close to $500. Now that is some serious money. And since I had already incorporated the "times twelve rule" into my life a long time ago, I knew that it was going to be somewhere around that number, and so the feeling was even better. I began this whole thing at a point where I struggled every month, where credit card companies were making loads of money off of me, and where I was wasting money at every turn. Now, I came to the point where I had enough money to put it somewhere and actually generate extra income for me. Not to steal a line from Visa or anything, but that feeling was "priceless."

Currently, I have about three to four of these types of things going on in my life where my money is generating more income for me. Some generate more than others, but to get to this point from where I was just several years before was, again, priceless.

Mid-2000 to now—not cheap, but savvy

It seems that we've come full circle now, haven't we? From mid-2000 to now, I would have to say that I've been in my current state of mind. I am sure that there are some people in my life who see the way I live and some of the things that I do and probably call me cheap behind my back. Guess what? I could care less. They can call me anything that I want. I have nice clothes to wear when I go out, my wife and son are very well provided for, and when I eat out I always leave a good tip. Small examples, but I know in my heart that I am not cheap. And even if I was, who cares? I can tell you one person that doesn't and that is me. If that is all that I have to put up with in order for me to get my financial house in order, then so be it.

My point is that I do not consider myself to be cheap, I consider myself to be savvy, and there is a big difference.

ALERT:

There is a big difference between being "cheap" and being financially "savvy."

Cheap is, among other things, not wanting to pay your share of the bill when you go out with friends, or simply not going out at all because you don't want to spend money. Cheap is hoarding all of your money for a rainy day that you know will never come and never enjoying the money you make. Being financially savvy, however, is completely different. Being financially savvy means checking my bills every month for errors and fighting to get them corrected (and you will find errors and sometimes you will have to fight to get them corrected). We will discuss this later, too.

Financially savvy means being able to get that new portable DVD player for $39.99 and instead of $59.99, which is the price you found it for at the first place you looked. Being financially savvy means doing things in your everyday life that involve nothing more than changing a habit of yours that will result in saving money. Being financially savvy also means keeping track of where your money goes and eliminating things in your life where you are spending money unnecessarily. I guess what I am trying to do is to wrap up all of the things that I now do in my life to save as much money as I can, to spend as little as I can on the things that I buy, and more importantly now, to find as many ways as possible to generate more income in my life (without changing jobs or careers, that is).

Basically, that is what I do now and have been doing for the last several years. Oh, another thing. You may wonder how much time this takes out of my life. Guess what? Not much at all. So many of these things are part of my daily/weekly/monthly routine that the actual time I invest in it now is minimal. Of course, it did take a while to set some things up, but if you think I stay awake until four in the morning staring at my computer till my eyes are bloodshot trying to save twenty-five cents on a gallon of milk, you are wrong. It is not like that at all. I am not fanatical about this whole thing, and it does not take a lot out of my week or month. Because I can tell you another thing. Anything that I feel does take too much time and is not worth the money I get out of it, I stop doing. More about this later. Yes, there are some things that I know that I could do that would generate money for me in my life that I choose not to do. Do you know why? The biggest reason is that right now I have a two-year-old son who wakes me up every off day and wants to play the whole day. This little boy and the time that I get to spend with him are more important to me than just about anything else in my life. Of course, I still find time to do things that make money for me, because I know that this in turn will help me provide a better life for him, but I also don't let some things get in the way of my time with him. If a certain endeavor or project or whatever does not meet my "time/cost effectiveness threshold," I stop doing it. This is a very important concept for me and one that I am near and dear to.

I will give you a short, quick example. If there was a portable DVD player that I wanted to buy, and I could save $20 on it by driving thirty minutes further down the road to buy it from another store, I would do it in a heartbeat. However, if there is something that I can do on the Internet that will take one hour of my time and generate $5 for me, then I would either not do it or stop doing it. A good example of this is surveys that you can fill out on the Internet for money. I used to be on a few different Web sites that were sending me surveys all the time. Guess what? A lot of them were not generating much money at all, some none. I soon eliminated all of those that weren't worth it to me, and now I fill out surveys from two sites only. Where do I determine the cut off? I look at how much money I can make and how long it will take me. Then, as a sort of yardstick, I look at how much money I currently make per hour at my job. If any particular project can make me more than my hourly rate for one hour of work, then I usually do it. If it falls below that number, I usually scrap it.

The point I am trying to make is that all of the things that I do on a daily or weekly basis do not consume my life, and they don't take away from my time with my family. If you get to the point in your life where you do have extra money that you can enjoy, but you never have the time to enjoy it, then what's the point?

What I do now is continue to look for ways to save money in my everyday life, and believe me, I can still find them. Also, ever since I got a personal computer at home, I would say that this dramatically sped up my entire timetable of getting to the point where I am now. Anyone who does not have a PC at home is out of his mind. Used for the correct purposes, it is my firm belief that a PC can pay for itself in about the first six months of ownership, and generate you much more money in the long run than you ever originally paid for it. The amount of research that you can do to impact these areas of your life and the speed with which you can do them has been an immeasurable part of my success since I first got mine in 2000. I probably won't mention this anywhere else, but if you are at some stage of financial difficulty in your life and you don't have a computer at home, one of the first investments you need to make as soon as you can make it is a personal computer. And guess what? If you know where to shop for them, you can get one at a very reasonable price—a lot less than you probably think.

ALERT:

If you do not have a personal computer at home, you need to invest in one as soon as possible. It will speed up the whole process like you would never believe.

There you have it! My story, basically, from beginning to end. So where, exactly, am I right now? I will tell you. I am writing this book in my spare time, I get paid a decent salary at my regular job, my wife does not work, and as I have said, I have a two-year-old son at home. I pay all of my bills every month, I think my family lives a very comfortable lifestyle, and

I think that I am well invested enough that if I continue to do so, I should be OK for my retirement. As far as I can tell, that is about the life of a "regular Joe," except for "regular Joe" probably does not save as much money as I do, he probably does not spend as little money as I do on the things that I buy, and he is probably not able to generate as much money as I am in my spare time. No offense meant to "regular Joe."

I'll be perfectly honest with you. One of the reasons I decided to write this book was based on trying to generate more income in my daily life without switching careers or jobs or anything else. Of course, I want to help people and I think that I have a lot of good information and good ideas to offer. But, of course I'd like to make some money doing it too. Who wouldn't? You may even notice by the price you paid for this book that I am trying to help you. That is, of course, unless you got a good deal on it already by buying it used or through an online site rather than going to a book store!

CHAPTER 2

The Mental Aspect and Approach

"If you would be wealthy, think of saving as well as getting." -
Ben Franklin

As I said, I basically hit rock bottom as far as being in debt and I knew I needed to do something in a hurry. To be honest with you, this decision was basically made for me. The reason I say that is because for the most part, I *couldn't go into debt any further than I already was.*

The credit card companies had already closed most of my credit cards and I had long since lost the ability to ask my parents to borrow money. How else could I get more in debt? I had to do something.

This is where my mental approach began. I certainly did not sit down one day and write down:

"OK, from this day forward I will have willpower and I will change my thoughts on money."

No, to the contrary. I simply started to do it. And this is how I would suggest starting to you. As is with anything in life, it is all about the starting. Let's pause for a second:

ALERT:

As with anything in life, it is all about getting started. Take that step, take some action, and soon everything else will fall into place.

I could compare it to a diet or an exercise program or quitting smoking or anything else like that. I just had to get started. And that's what I did. I don't know exactly what the first step was, but I do remember that I told myself that I needed to stick with this until the end. The motivation for this was because I knew that if I didn't, that I would be struggling financially for the rest of my life. But what also provided further motivation for me and something that I will mention countless times in this book, is that the sacrifices that I made I knew would not have to be forever. I think that's where a lot of people get lost and lose hope. If you think that you won't be able to ever attend a baseball game again (or whatever it is that you genuinely enjoy doing), then you're likely to lose hope. Instead, tell yourself that, OK, you might not be able to go to any baseball games this summer until you get your act together. (I only use this example because I am a huge baseball fan). And you might have to tell yourself that the next summer and maybe even the next summer. Or maybe you'll tell yourself that you can only go to two games this year when normally you would attend ten. My point is that you do not necessarily have to employ the "cold turkey" approach to everything in your life, and also that the sacrifices that you do make, for the most part, are going to be on a temporary basis. This was a key to keeping on the right path. It also allowed me to enjoy these things that I had given up so much more when I was able to do them again without feeling bad about the money I spent on them.

The way I maintained my willpower throughout it all was to develop the motivation to stay on track. That's what worked for me and I know it can work for you. Again, there WILL be some sacrifice involved in this whole thing. If you really want to do this, you will probably have to give up some things in your life for a certain period of time. What you need to remember is that these sacrifices are not permanent. This should provide further motivation. (Some things you will actually only give up for thirty days, or maybe sixty days. We'll get to that a little later.) Additionally, once you get started on this, you will realize that the whole process is a lot less about sacrificing than it is about changing your thoughts and attitudes towards money and changing behaviors and habits in your life. Trust me, this helps a lot also, because changing a habit or behavior in your life is a lot easier than giving something up for a decent period of time.

I don't get into any specific sacrifices that one would need to make in this book because I think they are different for all of us. And, if you sit down and think about it, it should not be that hard at all to figure out what they are. Should you sacrifice ten things in your life all at once? Probably not. You'd probably be back to square one in a hurry. That is another point that needs to be made. *There is no timetable.* At least there was not for me. I was just in a financial mess and I knew I needed to get out. Simple as that. Obviously, the more sacrifices you make and the more behaviors you can change, the quicker it will all happen, but I would not worry about that at the beginning. The first providers of motivation will be when you first start to see tangible results in your personal economy—at least that's what it was for me. As soon as I began to see things getting better in my life financially, it motivated me to expand the entire endeavor and increase my willpower, and drive me to change more things in my life. It becomes a self-fulfilling prophecy.

That is probably about it on willpower and motivation. The biggest thing is to get started. Get STARTED; stick with it till you begin to see some results, and everything else should fall into place.

I think I have already said that it is more about changing your attitudes and habits towards money than it is about actual sacrifice. In order to show you how it all worked for me, I think it is important to look at some of the ways that I "previously" viewed money and spending. That is, how I looked at things before I "woke up" financially. When I stopped "being a mule."

Again, it was not like one day I woke up and I said to myself, "David, you need to change your attitudes and habits towards money." No, not at all. I think it just happened after I finally made the decision to do something about my debt. It is really only looking back on things now that I learned about how I used to think about money (and how I used to spend it) and how I did through my little journey, and how I do now.

Did some of these changes occur over the course of time simply through the fact that I became a more mature individual? Certainly. But I also could have made these changes at a younger age (or instilled the correct beliefs about money in the first place) and I could have avoided a great deal of financial "wallet-ache."

Here are some of the ways that I previously thought about, or used to spend my money that directly led to a lot of my financial issues. I would imagine that some of these thoughts and attitudes will be quite familiar to you.

It was "cool" to blow money.

This part really came about after I got my credit cards. After all, you can't really "blow" cash unless you have it. When I had a few fresh credit cards in my pocket, I used to think it was "cool" to blow money.

Whether it was a night on the town bar-hopping and eating at nice restaurants where I would just pay the bill for everybody (again, just to look "cool") or trying to impress a girl , this led to a lot of my problems. Obviously, I was not thinking about the fact that this money would actually have to be paid back. And as far as "impressing" girls at that point in my life, there is not one single person still remotely involved in my life today that I was busy throwing money at during that part of my life. Coincidence? Maybe, maybe not. I'll touch more on this topic in a minute.

I guess I just wasn't serious about money and did not realize the effects that wisely spending your money versus simply blowing it can have on your personal finances. I am not a psychiatrist so I cannot even begin to get into the "why" of this happening, it just did. Also, I do not want anyone to think that I am proclaiming that people should never go out and enjoy their money. Not at all. I guess the first thing that I would recommend is that you simply check to make sure that you have it to go out and enjoy, and are able to enjoy it without a guilty conscience.

I will give you a short example. I had a friend of mine that I was hanging out with at the time, and he got the brilliant idea of us getting a "joint" American Express card.

He fell in love with the card because there was no limit on it. I know a lot of this will sound stupid, but it's all true. As I am sure you know, the card has to be paid off entirely at the end of every month. Also, he just simply loved the fact that we would be able to carry (and "flash") an American Express card.

I don't know what I was thinking, but I went along with it. Before you know it, he and I were eating at nice restaurants and taking girls to nice clubs and so on and so forth, until the bill came after the first month. During this time he always paid and I never saw the receipts so I never knew how big the bill was that was racking up. After the first month's bill came to his house, he drove over to my house, and told me that he needed $300. I had no idea for what, that is, until he showed me the first month's American Express bill. In the span of one short month, he and I managed to charge $600 on this credit card. He and I were only in our mid-twenties, and we did not make very much money at our jobs, so $300 was a huge amount of money for me. Of course, I started arguing with him about we should have kept better track of things and not spent so much money and everything else, but at the end of the day, we still owed the money.

Eventually, I paid it, made him cancel the card, and didn't hang out with him for a few months. I did learn one thing out of that little story—if anyone was going to get me into debt further from that point in time on, it would be me and me personally, not anyone else. The lesson didn't help much, but at least I told myself that I would be driving my own financial bus.

The victim's mindset

This is another role that I used to play so well. I was behind on my bills and just about everything else in my financial life, so this is basically how my month went: I got paid every two weeks, so the check that I got that fell when my rent and car payment was due was mostly spent. Rent and my car payment, if I remember correctly, were about the biggest expenses in my life. So, there wasn't much I could screw up at that point in time. I don't know how I managed it, but I was at least always on time with my rent, and I may have been a little short from time to time on my car payments, but I made them on time throughout the whole thing. I guess that is one saving grace. It was the paycheck that fell in between rent where the "victim's" complex came in. I would get paid, cash my check, and go pay the people that I owed money to. During the course of this whole mess, I used to borrow money from my friends a lot. Not really borrow it, but I would owe a friend because he paid the last time we went out, or someone leant me some money so I could take a girl out or whatever. To make a long story short,

by the time I finished paying everybody, I had no money left
to get me through until the next paycheck. I worked at restaurants throughout most of this whole mess, so I did most of my
eating at the restaurant. So, thankfully, groceries weren't much
of an issue for me.

My point is that I used to have the reputation of someone
who *never had money*. It was insane, but true. I worked a lot and
I made good money for that point in time and for what I was
doing, but I never had money. I was always out partying with
my friends, I always dated a lot of girls and always took them
to nice places, but my closest friends and my family members
all knew that I was one broke son of a gun. And I played the
role perfectly. It helped me gain sympathy from those people
around me in a very stupid sort of way. It was an easy role to
play—the whole "woe is me" kind of thing.

"This is happening to someone else."

This would actually be better stated as the person who is
doing the spending on the credit card is not the person who
is going to have to deal with paying the credit card back. I
remember specifically thinking about this on many occasions.
At this point in my life, I was living in Florida. This probably
did not help my situation much because there is a lot to do in
Florida and there are also alot of beautiful women in Florida.
With me being young, male, and single, it was a recipe for
disaster, right? I remember countless occasions where I either
decided to go on a vacation at the last minute, or I would go to
the mall and decide on a whim to make some large purchase or
a variety of other things. I would pay for it with my credit card,
and somewhere in the back of my mind something nagged at

me about who was really going to pay for it. I think a part of my brain actually thought that someone else would be paying for it. At least, that's how I thought because no matter what the cost was, the "paying back" part was certainly not at the forefront of my mind.

This is an easy game to let your mind play with you, but an expensive one. YOU are the one who has to pay all of this back. Unless of course you are lucky enough to have someone in your life who will pay your bills for you. But if this person does exist in your life, then you probably don't need to be reading this book.

This brings me to my next alert:

ALERT:

If you cannot afford to pay something back by the time your credit card is DUE, then you cannot afford to buy it.

Think about it. If you buy a flat screen TV for $1,000 and you can't pay it back by the time your credit card is due, then you have basically taken out a loan to buy the television. If you actually had to go to the bank, fill out an application, then wait for the credit check and the approval process, would you go through all of that just to be able to buy the TV? Probably not. By the way, your credit card company will probably charge you triple what a bank would charge to borrow the money. If you can begin to look at things in this fashion, it seems to me that you would be well on your way to reducing and ultimately eliminating most or all of your credit card debt.

The Opposite Sex

Finally, this was probably one of my most expensive negative attitudes about money and, I guess, life. When I was at this age, I loved dating women and lots of them. I would have a regular girlfriend but never really for more than a few months. I don't know why, that's just the way it was. Of course I used to try to "woo" women with my charm and "good looks," but in all honesty, I was never much of a charmer and if you've ever seen me, I'm not too high in the looks department either. So guess what I defaulted to as a way to gain and impress women? Money, of course. Now, this is no statement on my views of women or anything else, but I used to love to throw money at women to impress them and, hopefully, to ultimately win them over.

Now, if the "money-throwing" part had ended after I was able to win them over, that would have been great. But it always seemed to work out that for any of the women that I really had to throw money at to win over, I had to *continue* to throw money at them to keep them.

My point is this: If you have to throw money at a woman or a man in order to win them over, chances are that you are going to have to continue to throw money at them in order to keep them. This can get to be expensive. Plus, if you are looking for a life partner, wouldn't you really rather have someone that loves you for you rather than for your wallet?

I don't know—maybe my way of getting women back then was a reason why I never had a girlfriend for longer than a few months. Oh well, I had fun.

Let's move on to my more current and modern views of money. I am sure that some of these previous views came with my youth, but I also want to point out that I was still knee-deep in debt when I was thirty years old, so a lot of this has nothing to do with age or maturity; it was a conscious decision to change my outlook.

It's yours; treat it that way

So many times, I see people with what I know is some subconscious belief that their money, the money that they work for, is somehow simply destined to go to someone else and they will never get to a point in time in their lives when they can actually keep a larger percentage of the money that they make. I used to be the same way, and it is kind of similar to the "victim's" complex. Once I got out of debt and I had more money in the bank and more leftover after bills were paid, I really started to realize the importance of viewing it as something that is really mine. Another phrase comes to mind that really irritates me: "It's only money." Yes, that is absolutely true and nowhere in this book do I suggest or will I ever suggest that you become a slave to your money. Never do I advocate that. And if I come across that way it is not intended.

But if you treat something as actually yours, what do you tend to do? My first guess would be that you would take better care of it. Have you ever rented a car before? What is the thought going through the back of your mind? If you're a guy, it's probably something like, "Man, I am going to beat the crap out of this car while I have it since it's not mine and I just have to return it in one piece." I now treat my money much more like it is actually mine rather than like a rental car.

Not as something you continually give to others (victim complex)

This is simply elaborating on a point I touched on just before, but I feel it bears repeating. You need to get the victim mode out of your head and start to get more protective of your money. I will go much deeper into how to deal with companies that don't want to treat you fairly or actually try to take your money for no good reason, but to use a unique comparison: you need to become more like a protective mother bear with your money rather than a lazy cat. The mother bear won't let you near her cubs without a good reason, whereas a cat is likely to simply fall asleep rather than do much of anything. Wake up—realize that your money is actually yours and get rid of the victim complex.

Don't forget—you work hard for it (hopefully)

This is another thing that never really occurred to me during those years I was hopelessly in debt and couldn't get out. The fact is that I worked, and still do work, hard for my money. Hopefully this is true for you also. I sincerely hope that you do work hard for your money. If you don't, maybe you should consider starting and you might see your employer actually more willing to give you more of it, if you know what I mean. But that is also for another section of this book. Anyways, when I finally realized the fact that I do work hard for my money, then it gave me even more motivation in a variety of areas. It motivated me to take better care of it (my money, that is), it motivated me to get more upset when people tried to unfairly take it away from me, and I think this was really the advent of the "work week theory" that I came up with in my life and still use today. Which also led to the creation of my "hourly wage principle". This is how it all happened:

There was some point in time where I either wasted a good bit of money by missing a credit card payment, or I paid way too much for an item because I didn't do any research. Or maybe I just got a speeding ticket or something. I can't remember exactly what it was, but it occurred after I was almost completely out of debt and I had basically changed my views on money. For this example, let's say that it was a $200 mistake that I made. Well, I had already had most of my new positive views on money, so I was pretty upset about it. Had it happened long ago, I probably would have relished in being able to tell the story to my friends and family so they would feel sorry for me or my friends would think I was cool or whatever. But this time around it really upset me. Actually, it pissed me off. After I finally gave up trying to think of any way to undo what had happened, I started really thinking. At that point in time, I think my take home pay from my job was a little over $400 per week. Actually, I think it was more, but again, for this example, let's say my take home pay was exactly $400. Well, if you follow along that process, it doesn't take a rocket scientist to figure that I either just worked about half of a work week for free, or I was about to. Right?

As you can see, I was good and upset now. I was so mad at myself that I actually remembered this all of the next week at work. I thought about it all day Monday (which I worked for free) all day Tuesday (again free) and from 9:00 a.m. until about 1:00 p.m. on Wednesday also, because it was all free work. I think I only really started to settle down mentally later on during Wednesday when I was actually making money again.

I may be dramatizing my emotions and this story a little, but maybe this drama needs to be in your life to help you understand the big picture. Let me repeat—

IT'S YOUR MONEY—TREAT IT THAT WAY.
DON'T GIVE IT AWAY (BLOW IT) UNNECESSARILY.
YOU WORK HARD FOR IT, TRY NEVER TO WORK
FOR FREE!

I even began to apply this principle for smaller so-called "mistakes." Actually, it might be better to call them "missed opportunities." I remember a time when I purchased something, maybe it was a flat-screen TV (You see? I still do enjoy my money!). I bought it and then found out a few days later that I could have gotten the exact same television for $50 less somewhere else. I think it cost me around $400, and my first thought was, "Oh well, it's only fifty bucks from a $400 purchase—no big deal." And then I thought, "You know what? Fifty dollars is still fifty dollars, no matter how much the actual purchase was." I think my take-home pay was about $500 a week at that point, so that was about a half of a free work day. When I looked at it like that, I didn't get as pissed off as I did about the $200 example, but it put things in a much more proper perspective. Had I taken oh, about thirty extra minutes or so in my research than I did before buying the TV, I could have actually been paid for those four hours that I worked. Let's see, invest a few minutes for four paid hours of work. Sounds like a no-brainer to me. So, the "work week theory" and the "hourly wage principle" go hand in hand. I define more clearly all of these terms and concepts later on in the book

Another example. Did you suddenly decide to stop paying attention to your power usage around your house? Leave lights on unnecessarily? Have open windows during the summer time? Did maybe your power bill increase by $25 before you realized what was happening? Well, there you go. On Monday, when you go back to work, forget about getting paid until around 11:00 a.m., because you just wasted that money. Now, with all of these examples that I am bringing up on all these different topics—researching purchases, turning off lights and everything else, you may think I am a miser of some sort, I am a slave to my money, and I spend all my free time micromanaging my daily routine to try to save money. Well, that is just not true. I simply put all of these thoughts and ideas into place, turned them into habits, and now I don't really spend much time at all on these things. I need every extra minute I can get in my life with a two-year-old son at home!

A few more quick examples. Maybe you're not quite as organized with respect to paying your bills as you should be, and you missed a credit card payment. Well, with late fees and interest rates what they are these days; this can cost you upwards of $100 depending on your situation. In that case, your whole Monday's pay just went to someone else for no good reason at all.

Or let's say you notice a mistake on one of your utility bills. Let's say it is in the amount of $75. Does this happen a lot? Probably not. The first thing you need to do is to make sure you are checking these bills for these mistakes and the second thing to do is when you notice them, DO SOMETHING ABOUT IT! Have you ever found something like this and were either too afraid or too lazy to get it fixed? That happened to me before, but that goes back to my old way of thinking about money. With my new money habits, I tell myself, I don't owe this money, I am not going to pay it, and I will do what is necessary to get it fixed. We'll talk much more later on in the book about how to take on utility companies, or credit card companies, or whoever. Many times, these people are nice about these things and fix them for you without a lot of drama and effort. But sometimes, they're not. And there is a right way and a wrong way to go about handling this.

With respect to my credit cards, by the time I was five or six thousand dollars in debt, I always remember reading the statements when they came in. They would have finance charges on them ranging from about $50 up to about $200, depending on the card. I always remember looking at these numbers and saying, "Well, since I owe them $2,000, this extra $200 isn't that bad."

This is where I was wrong. What I should have thought was—this is $200 that I am just giving away.

What I also should have thought was—since I am making about $7 per hour at my current job, the first 28.5 hours that I work every month is basically for free! (My "hourly" rule in action.)

The third thing I should have thought was—I am pissed off! I work hard for my money and the last thing I need to be doing is to give it away to somebody.

Now, I'd like to give you a few concrete examples of how I started changing my financial health.

One of the first is the creation of my "thirty-day trial" concept. It is basically exactly what it sounds like.

It has a lot to do with the "sacrifice" part that I spoke about earlier. I think that one of the main reasons that these things succeeded for me, and definitely the main reason why they STILL work for me today when I use them (yes, I still find new ways to save money even now) is that I did not tell my brain that I was giving up whatever I was giving up forever; as a matter of fact, I started out with only thirty days. Again, I don't think I can emphasize this enough. As a matter of fact, we'll even make an alert out of it.

ALERT:

When instituting this system and changing your mindset about money, how you spend it and how you save it, the "sacrifice" part of the whole thing is not as terrible as it sounds. Use the thirty-day trial.

Let's start off with a small, but probably very relevant example for most of us. A few days after I started my journey down Savings Lane, I remember stopping at a gas station to get gas and then running inside to get a Coke, like I always used to do. As I told myself that I was going to begin analyzing as many parts of my life as I could to identify ways to save money, I thought to myself: "Wow, I wonder how much money I could save if I stopped drinking Coke." I think most of us know that it's not very good for our insides no matter how good it tastes, and I figured I could probably save a lot of money. I decided to myself that I would stop buying a Coke at the gas station whenever I filled up for a period of thirty days, and if I missed it too much (actually, if I didn't have enough willpower) then

I would simply put that idea aside and try to come up with other ways to save money.

I soon came to the conclusion that it was not necessary to *completely* stop drinking Coke, just to eliminate the part of my routine where I got one every time I filled up my tank. I told myself that I wouldn't STOP drinking Coke, I'd just stop getting it at the convenience store. If I really needed that Coke, I could get a twelve-pack from the grocery store for probably the same price as about three individual Cokes at the convenience store, and just carry one with me. Then I could always drink a Coke in the car, if this "sacrifice" thing got to be too awful.

In the beginning, I did miss my Cokes at the gas station. But I told myself it was only for thirty days, and every time I'd get the urge to stop and get a Coke, I'd simply remind myself to go to the grocery store and pick up a twelve-pack. Well, I never remembered my reminders, and within a few weeks, I really didn't miss my Cokes at all.

So guess what? It turned out to barely be a *sacrifice* at all! It was in reality just a change in habit. I never really missed out on the joys of drinking Coke; I just waited until I got to work and drank one for free. It never got to the point where I had to stock up my fridge with Cokes so I could carry one with me. It was all just a change in habits. By telling my mind that it would originally only be for thirty days, I was able to make this change in habit.

On a side note, I eventually gave up drinking Coke entirely because of other reasons (health and diet). I don't know if that saved me even more money (I am sure it did because now instead of ordering Coke at restaurants, I simply order water, which is free), but it ended up being a huge win-win for both my wallet and my body.

Of course, I am not telling everyone to give up drinking Coke. If you like to drink it, go right ahead. I am simply showing you that the whole "sacrifice" part of things can really be minimized with the use of my "thirty-day trials" and a lot of times, things merely turn out to be a change of habit rather than any sort of serious "sacrifice."

Let me give you another, even better example. When I began my crusade to end my financial stress/woes/misery, another one of the things that I looked at was my electric bill. At the time, I was living in a one-bedroom apartment and I believe my electric bill was somewhere around $75 per month. I already knew as soon as I started to think about this topic that I should be able to seriously impact my savings in this area. To begin with, my apartment was cooled by electricity in the summer and heated by gas in the winter, so this really only applied to the summer.

Before I seriously looked at this stuff, I had my thermostat set at seventy degrees for the entire day. Even though I left most of the time in the morning and worked all day, I just left it set at seventy the whole time. I guess I never really thought about it. It was just like that so when I came home in the evening, my apartment was at a comfortable level.

This example occurred a little further along in my whole "savings" crusade and this particular example hit me when I was getting particularly obsessive about saving money. This is what I decided: I would not only begin to set my thermostat at seventy-eight degrees rather than my amazingly comfortable seventy, but I would also simply turn off my air when I left my house in the morning and just turn it back on in the evening when I came home.

In the beginning, I endured it because I was adamant about saving money. But, a few things soon became quite apparent for me. First, seventy-eight degrees was waaaaaayyyyyyyyyyyyy tooooooooooooo hot! I just couldn't do it. I wasn't able to sleep at night, I was grumpy, and so on. Secondly, at the time I was still working in a restaurant. For any of you who have worked in restaurants, you know it is hard work, and a lot of the time, you are working in a hot kitchen. I would say that about ninety-nine percent of the time, I came home sweaty and tired. About the last thing I wanted or needed in my life was to come home to a steamy apartment and have to wait an hour or so for my apartment to cool down.

These two things just proved to be too much for me, and at first, I was tempted to just stop them. But again, like I said, this "thirty-day trial" thing did not come to me before I started any of my savings; it was part of the evolution of my behavior. In reality, it may have been this AC example that gave this "thirty-day trial" thing life (either that or Coke, I don't remember). As I sat there one night in my sweaty clothes waiting for my apartment to cool down, I just decided that there were other ways to go about saving money besides this one. But rather than completely scrapping the idea, this is what I decided to do.

Instead of going from the extreme of living in an apartment set at seventy all the way up to seventy-eight, I decided to just go up to seventy-two. Additionally, instead of completely turning off my air during the day time when I wasn't at home, I just raised the thermostat up to seventy-six. That way, when I came home I was not completely uncomfortable, and it really only took about twenty minutes or so for my apartment to cool back down (which was about how long it took for me to take a shower and change clothes anyways) and the seventy-two degree thing was really not very noticeable. I may have noticed it for the first few days, but after that, not at all.

Thus, the first summer I went from seventy to seventy-two. The next summer, I bumped it up another two degrees to seventy-four. Then, I bumped it up another degree each summer till I hit seventy-seven. Sorry, I couldn't and/or wouldn't go past seventy-seven. I did this till I was completely out of debt and well on my way to financial freedom. Then, I celebrated with a summer of seventy-four in my new home (until I got the sticker shock of the difference between an electric bill in a one-bedroom apartment compared to a 1300-square-foot home!), and I currently set my air at about seventy-six. It is hard to apply the "times twelve rule" to this example because other things affect your power bill, but the last year in my apartment, my electric bill was down around $40 to $45, so I saved about $30 from the beginning to the end. Multiply that by the nine summer months we have in Atlanta, and it was around $270 in annual savings. So, there you have it: a thirty-day trial and the times twelve rule working hand-in-hand.

I'd like to also talk a little bit about the importance of organization in your life if you are going to get serious about putting your finances in order. Up to this point in time in my life, bills were simply nuisances to me that I would get around to whenever I felt like it. I mean, c'mon, they're just bills and as long as you pay them before they cut your services off or before they close your account, who cares, right? (This goes back to taking ownership in the money you make.)

I felt this way for a lot of reasons. One, most utility companies really didn't even charge any kind of a late fee back in those days so those bills didn't even cost me any extra money if I paid them late, and with respect to the credit card companies, well, I owed them extra money anyway from the finance charges, so who cared if they tacked on a little bit more?

After I got serious about getting out of my mess, I kept hearing over and over again that paying your bills on time is important. And if you have ever looked at a copy of your credit report/credit score, you'll see why. For basically every single account you have, whether it is for a utility company or credit card, they have a section under each one with the number of times you paid your bill late, more than thirty days late, more than sixty days late and more than ninety days late. I don't know exactly what effect each of these individual breaches has on your score, but I know it's not good. I also know that once I had paid all of my bills on time for a period of six months that my credit score went up significantly.

The way you go about paying your bills on time is up to you, but it seems to me that it involves some type of organizational system. Back in the day before online bill paying and all the other conveniences that we have today, this meant that instead of dropping all my bills in a shoe box and getting around to paying them whenever I remembered to, I simply went out and bought a $3 calendar that I used for bill-paying dates only.

No birthdays or doctors' appointments or anything else on this calendar. Every time a bill came in the mail, I would write this down on my calendar *five days before it was due.* This would allow for mailing time and so on. Then, I simply prioritized it as part of my finances that I no longer put off paying a bill on time for anything else going on. My bills took first priority in my life. After six months, like I said, it had a significant effect on my credit rating.

Just to modernizeize things a little, I want to share with you my organizational system now. Before I was married and had children as I am sure you can guess, I had fewer bills and I had fewer accounts to pay. Back then I had it set up to where I paid my bills one time per month! Most of it just worked out that my bills had due dates either right around the end of the month or right at the beginning of the month, so I only had to go through this process one time per month. This eliminated the need for a calendar, and so I just tucked each bill inside my checkbook as it came in, and I knew that on the twenty-fifth of every month, I needed to set aside about thirty minutes to go on the computer and pay my bills. Now that I am married and have children, I have more bills to pay, and I now pay bills two times per month. There are about three that are due around the second week of the month and the rest at the end of the month. With small children at home, things just have a tendency of disappearing, so I also have a little Post-it attached to my checkbook that lists all of the bills that I need to pay on a monthly basis. Each time I sit down to pay bills, I cross reference this list to make sure that I don't miss a bill because my son threw it in the trash by mistake. Whatever system works for you organizationally is fine, but it seems to me that you'll need one in order to stay on top of this, and it is worth having one because staying on top of paying your bills on time is very much worth doing.

Now, this next part is more mental than anything, and as I recall, once I got started and started seeing some concrete results in my bank account, this whole thing just happened naturally. The idea is to basically start thinking about the subject more. When driving to work, waiting in line, doing whatever mindless drivel fills up our days, think. Think. How can I save money? Not necessarily what else can I sacrifice, but how can I "piss away" less money. If you leave the house with the lights on, you're pissing away money. Leave the AC set at sixty-five—pissing away. What I used to do from time to time when I was first getting into this was to simply go through my entire day and try to identify ways to save money. Most of it was quite a boring process, but you really do have to think. I never really realized that I could save money every time I put gas in my car until I realized that I didn't really need to buy that Coke. Leaving the AC on at a comfortable temperature so I would be nice and cool the second I opened my door in the evening never stood out to me as a waste of money until I actually thought about it.

Another way to start to get this mentality into your everyday life is to think about things as you are doing them (or, better put, "Stop Being a Mule"). I think that this method actually worked a little better for me because it was just too hard to think about all the little things that I do during the day and to analyze them as to how to save money. It was a lot easier for me to think about things as I was doing them. Let me explain. Most of the time we always have stuff on our minds.

We rarely, if ever, have absolutely nothing running through our brains. But I will pose this question to you: How often are the things that we have on our minds really so extremely important that there is not something more productive that we can think about? If you are on the way to an important job interview or have a big meeting with your bosses at work today, then you know what? Forget about thinking about ways to save money. However, if you are driving to work and thinking about tonight's football game, or thinking about what "cool" thing to say to some pretty girl at work, why not think about some ways to save money instead? That is, make a mental note to yourself to analyze things as you are doing them. Now, I do not want to get too psychologically deep about this or make this out to sound like it is some long and draining process, but this was a big factor in helping me personally to begin to save money. Analyze your daily life activities. When you are brushing your teeth, do you really need to leave the water running? Or better yet—when you are shaving? Probably not. If you use my "times twelve" rule with one of those examples, the dollar amount might be $10 over the course of a year, but you know what? Ten bucks is ten bucks. And you combine that with ten other little things that you can change in your daily routine and there you have it, you just saved yourself $100 in a year without basically doing anything but changing habits. And notice, I did not even mention sacrificing anything.

So, begin the "thought process" and I bet you will be shocked at what you can find. You can do just as much, if not more, in the area of lowering your expenses as you can in the area of trying to generate more income. Let me repeat that and make an alert out of it:

ALERT:

You can do just as much, if not more, in the area of lowering your expenses as you can in the area of trying to generate more income.

There is some saying out there that goes something like— no matter how much money you make, you'll still always spend it. Or something like, Even though you get a raise at work, you'll still blow through it. Let me tell you what, I could not disagree with that statement more. And I am living proof of that. I am here to tell you that once I started getting those decently sized bonus checks, my spending behaviors did not change one bit. My expenses did not go up—none of that happened. Do you know why? Because I was not in a position to do so, and I still had a long way to go. Again, it never really came down to sacrifice; it was a matter of willpower. And, once again, I had always told myself that life would not always be like that, and if I worked hard enough maybe the next time I got a good raise at work or a good bonus check, then maybe I could just go out and enjoy it.

Of course, I did treat myself a little. You may think this sounds stupid or crazy, but as I remember, my first good bonus check was about $800 (which was a ton of money for me at the time) and I think I treated myself by upgrading the thirteen-inch television set that I had with a twenty-four-inch TV. Yup, sure did. And you know what? I was the happiest guy on Earth with that TV (who wouldn't be?). A lot of you may be saying that there's no way I could have that much willpower, or this guy's an idiot for not at least enjoying some of that money, but guess what? I have a good bit of money that I am enjoying now and that I will enjoy for the rest of my life because of all that hard work and effort that I put in back then to fix my situation.

Now, to close out this section, I want to talk a little about what my mental outlook was throughout this whole process. We already talked about some of the mental concepts or ideas that you can adopt into your life. Well, here are some of the outlooks or attitudes that I took on which made this whole thing possible. Did you know that fixing or fine-tuning your finances has very little to do with how much money you *actually make,* and much more to do with *your mental outlook and your particular thoughts about* money? We've already spoken about a lot of it, but as I was writing this section, I tried to look back as to what exactly I was telling myself during these two to three years that allowed me to get the results that I did. Here is what I came up with:

Stick With It. If you decide to implement some or all or any of my ideas, you'll find that it is similar to starting a diet. The first few days of your 30-day trials, or new ways of thinking are where you will be tempted to go back to your old habits and just say forget about it. This is where most people do give up and where I gave up several times before I finally got serious. Here is what motivated me. When you are in debt (or when you don't have enough money to do the things that you want to do in life), it weighs on your mind constantly (i.e., the phone bill is due, or getting turned off, on Tuesday but I can't pay it till Friday so I have to call them and beg. Or, I spent too much money last weekend so I can only pay the minimum on my credit cards. Or, I need to take my car in for $300 worth of repairs and I have no idea how to pay for it). If you're just trying to fix your finances, your thoughts may be more like, if I only had a little more money I could do this, or I could buy that, or I could start my own business and get out of this job that I dislike, etc. The point is, those thoughts are there *constantly.*

Now, if you can make it past the initial stages of this new process, at least to the point that you see some results, you will get your own built-in motivation to continue on. By seeing these actual, real results in your life, and starting to realize what living life without all of these constant money thoughts bearing down on you is like is an amazing feeling. Those thoughts and those feelings were what it took for me to start looking for ways in every single facet of my life where I could either stop spending money unnecessarily, save money, or start to generate more of my own. What I am trying to say to you in a nutshell is that you have to stick with it. Of course it is going to be a little difficult in the beginning—what kind of change in your life isn't? Tough it out through the first thirty days or the first few months, and I promise you—once that first credit card is paid off and you no longer have to worry about it, or once you put a system in place to pay your bills on time every month, these gorillas that you peel off of your back one by one will give you an inner feeling like few others. After that it won't seem like sacrifice at all.

Put ON the Blinders. No matter how much you are in debt and no matter how many problems are arising from it, the first things you need to have are willingness and desire. I can show you all of the steps, but without these two, it won't work. There will be some sacrifices involved, but they will seem like nothing once you are firmly on your way to financial freedom. Of all the times in life where people are telling you to "take off the blinders," for once, here, you are being told to put them on. Take your sights off of short-term unnecessary purchases and little luxuries, and zero-in on the long-term goal—financial freedom. Now, I just finished telling you to forget about some short-term things and remember the long-term goal. Well, now in my next breath, I want to tell you the exact opposite. Yup, I also want to say that in one important aspect, you need to take your mind OFF of the long-term goal and simply focus on the short-term ones. What I mean by this is that if you are, say, $10,000 in debt, you need to completely forget about that number. If that is the number you are focusing on in the beginning, I feel there is no way that you can stick with it. In the beginning, you need to focus on your short-term goals that you've set for yourself (i.e., doubling the minimums on your credit cards, rolling the AC back two degrees, etc.). Thinking about that huge number in the beginning would kill anyone's motivation. So, yes, in some aspects you need to forget about the short-term stuff and focus on the long term, and in others, the complete opposite is true. This may be a little confusing or even a little hard to believe, but the only thing I can tell you is that it worked for me, and it has worked for a lot of other people who have taken my advice. So, if the number in your life happens to be $10,000 (in debt), forget about it and focus on what you can do in your life tomorrow to save some money. Keep in mind when to focus on the long term and also how not to become overwhelmed by it. It is a fine line but should become fairly easy with time.

Nothing Is Forever. When you focus on your monthly bills and saving money, keep in mind one thing—the changes you need to make do not have to be permanent. Maybe you'll decide to implement these changes for six months, maybe a year, maybe more. Maybe you'll decide to do it for one month just to see how it affects you. But always keep in mind that these changes do not have to be permanent. That thought always worked for me when I implemented them.

Now, as promised here is a little guide that simply re-hashes all of the concepts and terms that I came up with along the way...

My "Times Twelve" Rule

If I show you a way to lower a certain bill by $10 a month, or another way to save $10 a month, that may not seem like much to you or worth doing. However, if you look at these savings over the course of an entire year, using the "times twelve" rule, you will see that it will save you $120 on a yearly basis. That is much more motivating and much more worth doing. And then, to make it even more motivating, convert that into something else concrete. Tell yourself that if you put into place whatever that saving tip is and you do save the $120, then compare it to a free car payment (if your car payment is around $120) or, to two free power bills (if your bill is normally around $60). Putting these savings into annual terms and relating them to concrete expenses in your life will help you implement these changes in your life as well as stay motivated and committed to them.

Thirty-Day Trials

I instituted some things in my "personal economy" called a series of "thirty-day trials." What is a "thirty-day trial" you ask? Well, it is just what it sounds like. Just like those things you hear all over TV and radio about trying a certain product and if after thirty days you don't like it you can get your money back, I did the same thing, I just applied it to all of my spending.

What you need to do is to look at something that you think you could save money by eliminating in your life. It could be Cokes (which I already mentioned), maybe it's snack food, maybe it's cigarettes, it could be anything. Anyways, you know it is something that if you took out of your life you could save a lot of money, you just don't know how you're going to do it. That's when you decide to try it for thirty days. Make a note on your calendar thirty days from the date you start and tell yourself, I am giving it up till then. Also, in order to track it, I would try to find a way to see how much money you saved in those thirty days.

I think that anybody who has any willpower at all can go without something for thirty days without too much of a problem. What I found when I did this was that after the first few days, I was eyeing that circle on my calendar, desperately waiting for that thirtieth day to come so I could return to whatever it was that I gave up. After the first week, it was a little less, and then in most cases, I had forgotten when the thirty days was even up.

Of course, I know that everything does not go so easily. So, here is the second plan of attack. Let's say for example, the thing you are giving up for thirty days is cigarettes. Also, let's say just for example that you smoke a pack every other day, and a pack of cigarettes costs $4.

You make it through your thirty days and you want to say, forget this, I am dying for a cigarette, I'll save money some other way. OK, that's fine. But before you do, get out the calculator. You would determine that in those thirty days, you saved yourself $60, and if you employ the "times twelve" rule, that translates into $720 in annual savings.

That's a pretty strong number. It may motivate you to start another thirty-day trial, or at least stay on track. If this still doesn't work, try this. Since you just made it thirty days without a cigarette, you know you are capable. If you still can't give them up entirely, why not tell yourself, OK, now I am going to make a pack last me four days instead of two. Or at least three days. This way, you do not have to completely give it up, but you've made some progress, and have probably come a lot closer to the day when you can say good-bye to your particular thing forever.

Work/Time Theory

This is a concept that has become very near and dear to me, especially since the birth of my first child. Mostly, it has to do with the research and time involved in the "saving more and spending less" aspects of this book, and also a lot to do with the time involved in generating extra income in your life.

It is actually a fairly simple concept. Basically, as far as saving more money or spending less money, if something is going to take me a longer period of time than I am willing to do devote to it in order to save a very small amount of money, I usually elect to simply not do it. This is also where I firmly believe that I am absolutely NOT fanatical about this whole money-saving, finance thing. I guess you could probably let it dominate your life, and one could probably save even more money than I do in my daily life, but my question at the end of the day would be: What kind of life are you living?

Let me expand. Let's say for example, that you make $10 an hour at your job. To me, I use that as a benchmark against any project or any research or any money-saving idea that I might decide to take on. A great example would be clipping coupons. To be perfectly honest with you, I do not clip as many coupons as I probably could, and for a lot of very good reasons. Besides the fact that I don't really shop on Sundays and therefore don't really buy the Sunday paper, there are other reasons. But back to my example. You make $10 an hour at your job. You also find out that it takes one hour each Sunday to go through the Sunday paper and clip out all your coupons (we'll use an hour just as an example). Let's also say you figure out that you save an average of $5 per week with these coupons. By utilizing my Work/Time Theory, this wouldn't be what I would call a waste of time, but I feel I could use my time more effectively by simply doing other things. In my case, it would be spending more time with my son.

The reason I say this is that you would be better off volunteering for an extra hour at work each week because you would make more money. After all, your object is to generate MORE income in your spare time, right? Well, to me, that has always meant making more than what I make at my regular job.

One quicker example. In Chapter 5, I talk about filling out surveys on the internet to generate more cash in your life. In the beginning, I was probably a member of about five of these sites. However, it soon became apparent to me that most of them were not a very effective use of my time. With some, I would have to spend about five hours filling out surveys in order to get something, either cash or a gift card, that was worth $10 to me. Now, that is a clear waste of time to me. I would much rather be spending time with my son, or using that time to figure out other ways to generate more money in my life, than to just get $10 for five hours of my time.

I guess if you have plenty of extra time on your hands, and you think it is a good idea, then go right ahead. But this whole process and, to an extent, way of life can easily overtake you as a person if you allow it to. Once again, I do not think I am fanatical about it, and I certainly know how to balance the time I spend on it with the rest of my life.

Because I have applied my Time/Work theory to this situation as well. Basically, if I cannot generate at least as much income as I make at my regular job, then to me, it is not worth doing. I would rather spend the time playing with my son or talking with my wife. Now, how much of a commodity "free time" is in your life may dictate how you decide to rate this. If you are single and possibly somewhat "bored" in your spare time, maybe you will put the cutoff point at $10 per hour. Then again, maybe if spare time is at quite a premium in your life, maybe you will set the bar higher. It is entirely up to you. The point is that there are a lot of things that you can do in your life right now to help you actually put more money in your wallet. And with a lot of them you can start today.

CHAPTER 3

Saving Money in Your Everyday Life

*"Money and women are the most sought after and the least
known about of any two things we have." -
Will Rogers*

At my point of greatest debt, I owed credit card companies
somewhere in the range of $15,000 and I also owed my parents
about $10,000. After I finally decided to do something about
it, and I changed my attitudes towards money and spending
and material things, I was able to get completely out of debt in
right around three years.

Even if you do not find yourself as far in debt as I was, and
you are just looking for ways to save money, I feel that I can
provide you with some good tips and strategies. Because that
also had a lot to do with me getting out of debt.

You can implement as much or as little of this process into your life as you would like, but, all of the things that I will talk about are things that I did personally, and that I know have worked for countless other people, and all put together, allowed me to get out of debt, and to be well on my way to financial freedom.

The reasons that I am writing this book today, and also the reasons that I think that this book contains information that most other books on the subject don't, are many. If I did not mention it before, I think this book can help people because of three things: I have never worked in the financial services industry, I am not rich, and I never studied finance. Basically, what I am trying to say with those three statements is that I was and am just a regular guy. A regular guy who faced and still faces real-world, relevant problems that are probably faced by a lot of other people out there. This book is not filled with a bunch of book answers that you might get from some finance major (I had discussions with them and that's what I got), I certainly am not trying to sell you anything (which is what I got whenever I spoke to someone in the financial services industry), and finally, I earn about a middle-class income. I know that a lot of the issues that I confronted and eventually conquered are also faced by a lot of other people in this country.

I invite you to read as much or as little of this book as you would like, page through and pull out the parts you need if you want. I wrote this book only to re-tell my story and only because I thought it could help other people.

Before I get into any specific categories of how to save money in your everyday life, I want to share with you a wildly simple concept that depending on your level of spending can make a serious dent in what you buy on a monthly basis. Again, it is quite simple.

It is a sure-fire way to help you save more money. Every time you go to take out your purse, or your wallet (and this goes for whether paying by cash or credit card, because it's the same thing), you need to ask yourself a very serious question: "**Do I really need this?**" Example—you are out of gas. Well, obviously, you NEED to put gas in your car. So, fill up your tank, go inside and pay, and leave. What that means is that the Coke you might want to buy or chewing gum or whatever else is in there that you have been buying in the past you probably don't NEED. This is a small example, but a good one. And not to belabor the point, but you need to ask yourself this question seriously. I could not put a dollar figure on it, but I know that adopting this concept into my life has made a huge impact on my financial situation over the years. It certainly went a long way in helping me get out of the mess that I was in, and it also helps me keep my spending in line to this day. Of course, this does not apply to after you've seen some real results in your financial life. At that point, I say go ahead and treat yourself to something nice. There is no point in going through this whole exercise if you are not going to reward yourself at certain points along the way. But by asking yourself the "Do I really need this" question each time you get ready to spend, you can seriously impact the way that money is currently going out of your life.

Let's move on to some specific ways to save more money in your everyday life.

Credit Card Debt

This is where it all started with me. The area of credit card debt is so broad and so vast that it is impossible to discuss every area of it in one chapter. However, I can provide you with a few key points that should give you some hope. No matter how large or small your credit card debt is, I can give you some strategies that have been proven to work (I know so because I developed them myself and they have worked for me and many others) and it costs you nothing extra. Which is my way of telling you that you should never contact one of these companies that offers to consolidate your debt for you because no matter how they dress it up, *they are not saving you money, they are costing you money.*

I also want to tell you that it has very little to do with how much money you make or how much you are in debt. It has a lot more to do with your willingness and desire to get out of debt and your attitudes towards money in general.

The first thing that needs to be done is that we need to start emptying the tub rather than filing it up more. You are probably asking yourself what in the world I am talking about. When I finally decided to take on my credit card debt and fix it once and for all, for some reason I compared it to a bathtub full of water. Actually, I think that one night right around the time I decided to get serious about this stuff, I had been running a bath for myself, and inadvertently forgotten about the running water. By the time I remembered it, there was water spilling all over my bathroom floor.

The metaphor was obvious to me. It's the first thing that I thought of. I said, "Goodness, this kind of reminds me of my credit card debt."

That visual image stuck with me the entire time I was in debt with my credit cards.

Let's take a look at this. The water in the bathtub is your credit card debt. We need to reduce it. What are the two ways you can reduce the amount of water in a bathtub? One, you can stop adding water from the faucet, and two, you can open up the drain to let it out the bottom of the tub.

This is how you need to attack (yes, attack!) your credit card debt. That is what I did. We do it in two ways. We turn the faucet off, first. And second, we drain as much water as we can out of the bottom until the bathtub is dry. That is what we want—a dry bathtub (which means—no credit card debt!).

How do we turn off the faucet? In the beginning, you prob-ably want to consider cutting up your credit cards, putting them in the freezer —locking the faucet in the "off" position. If you are unable or unwilling to go that far, or you do have a legitimate need for your credit cards on a monthly basis, here is the next best thing, and the only real option to get you out of debt.

It is what I call the Golden Rule of Credit Cards:

IF YOU CAN'T AFFORD TO PAY FOR YOUR PURCHASE BY THE TIME THE BILL COMES—YOU CANNOT AFFORD IT. PERIOD.

Not to sound like a broken record, but so much more of this process is mental rather than actual concrete steps that you can take to impact your personal economy. It was not like I had a laundry list of things to do to get out of credit card debt and

I crossed them off one by one. Much to the contrary. As I stated before, the biggest thing is to change your mentality towards money, and with respect to credit cards, with spending. One day, I just decided my new mentality regarding my credit card debt was going to be "Attack, attack, attack," and I would do it with dogged determination.

To start draining the tub, I decided I was going to double the minimums on all of my credit cards. Before, I was lucky if I paid the minimum, and paid it on time. So, doubling them was a major step. Of course, you may say that you are in no financial position to even be able to afford doing something like this, but guess what? If you start to make some of the other changes in your life that I have already talked about and will talk about more later in this book, you will start to see a little extra money in your wallet or bank account . Once you see this, it is important to apply this to your credit card debt. So you see, most of the things that I talk about in this book are inter-related.

Second, if for some unbelievable reason I came across some extra money in one particular month (I don't know, maybe a birthday gift check from a relative or a rebate check from a utility company,) I shot that straight to a credit card without even thinking about spending it on something else.

To stop the tub from filling up, obviously, you have to decrease your credit card spending as much as possible. Of course, there is the golden rule of credit cards I listed above, but there is another question that you need to ask yourself while you are in the process of eliminating your credit card debt. And it is really a very simple question:

Do you really need it?

I know I just spoke about this a few pages ago, but it bears repeating and discussing a little further in detail. Yes, it is a very simple question. But with me, this was one of the main reasons why I got so deep into credit card debt. It came from buying things I didn't really need.

You just need to seriously ask yourself this question before you decide to whip out the plastic for anything. If it is for groceries, then yes, you probably need them. If it is for a shirt you saw in some store that you really like, guess what? You can probably do without it. The examples here could really be anything, but they mostly pertain to what I used to call my "weaknesses." It doesn't really matter exactly what they are, everybody has them. Simply put, you cannot give in to your weaknesses until you have at least shown some positivity in your process.

To simplify it further, in the beginning, I basically spent nothing on my credit cards. I walked past all of the shirts and all of the other things that I really didn't need, and simply tried not to buy anything. Don't worry, it is not that scary of a concept and it is not something you'll need to practice forever.

After doing this for about six months, and after seeing some MAJOR progress in my credit card balances, I think I went out and bought one of those shirts. You of course have to give yourself little treats along the way—little rewards, I guess you could call them. Remember, this whole thing is not about total and complete sacrifice, rather just changing your mindset about money and spending.

I would also try to stay away from actually looking at your credit card balances in the beginning. With me, the balances were so sky high that I never ever thought I would get out from underneath them. This is exactly the reason why you should try not to look at them. In a sense, you need to put ON the "blinders" (like I said before). There are so many examples in life where people tell you to take OFF the blinders, but in this example you really need to try to put them on.

Actually, it is a fine line to cross. Yes, you want to keep your eye on your long-term goal of getting completely out of debt, but you also need to stay away from focusing too much on the end game in the beginning or else you're likely to lose hope and give up. A quick example. I had one credit card balance which was almost $4,000. Of course, this wasn't the only one, this was just the highest that I remember. I don't remember the finance charge or the minimum payment on it, but I can tell you I was barely making it. When I finally got serious, I think I got my income tax return check and I decided to send $500 to all of my credit cards. Well, when you see your balance go from $4,000 down to what, maybe $3600 after the finance charge is taken out, your reaction, or at least mine, was something like—big deal. So what. So you should really stay away from focusing in on those balances in the beginning. If you stick with it, soon enough they will be back down into this hemisphere, and before long, they will be gone! For each credit card, I gave myself a little celebration when I cut the balance in half. When I got the one from $4,000 down to $2,000, I treated myself to a dinner at a nice restaurant. When I got another one from $3,000 down to $1,500, I went to a baseball game. Like I said, you have to treat yourself a few times along the way.

That is the majority of the advice I can give you about credit card debt. Again, it is not so much about doing A, B, C, D, and E and bam, you're out of credit card debt. It is much more about changing those mindsets and habits about money in general and especially about spending money. Now this may not be the most comprehensive advice in the world on credit card debt, but it is really all that I did to eliminate mine.

Grocery Shopping

So, ready for your regular weekly trip to the grocery store? Tired of the grind of going every week? Want to make it a little more fun and challenging? How about we start a little contest to see how much money we can save on a weekly basis? Sounds like it could be fun and profitable at the same time.

I think that it is safe to say that for most people or most households, groceries are probably the second biggest monthly expense, falling in right behind your mortgage/rent and right in front of your car payment(s) or somewhere close. Therefore, it stands to reason that this is one of the areas that if you concentrate, organize yourself, and do a little planning, that you can have a pretty big impact on your wallet. Make sense?

Before we begin, yes I am a guy and yes, I really do the majority of the grocery shopping for our household. Let's just say I took it on as a little project and it became a challenge.

What I want to do is to go through about five basic concepts that I put to use on a weekly basis, that when all added up, probably save me a ton of money at the grocery store(s).

And these concepts go a long way under the category of not "being a mule."

Expand your base…

You probably don't need to limit yourself to doing ALL of your shopping at one outlet. Personally, I use four. This will not take your grocery shopping from an hour or so a weekday night to a six-hour marathon—I still do not spend much more time doing it on a weekly basis.

Basically, what I do is to use one outlet (I won't name them) for the majority of my stuff and a second outlet that has items for a cheaper price. Third, I utilize a local farmer's market as much as possible. There should probably be one close enough by you and they are definitely worth checking out. Major savings! Most of the time the quality is just as good if not better than a major grocer and it is always at substantially cheaper prices. I cannot emphasize this point enough. Currently, I probably buy 70% of my items at my farmer's market. Typically, their prices on produce are substantially cheaper than anywhere else, but their prices on everything else are substantially higher. Therefore, just stick to buying veggies there. And finally, I do use a specialty store to treat myself every once in a while. You have to do that every so often throughout this process of revamping your finances, or you're liable to give up.

What I do with my second outlet is to utilize it for items I buy consistently that has them for less. This will take some time in the beginning but becomes easier as you go along. Here, you really just have to pay attention to the items that you buy the most. If you can find a store that sells something for fifteen cents cheaper, but you only buy it once every three months, then who cares? However, if you can find another store that you can save fifty or sixty cents on ten different items that you buy every week, then it becomes worth doing. I wouldn't know if this concept applies to everyone since we all have different buying habits, but it works for me.

Couponing...

One important concept to couponing is the importance of using one main store, and using it consistently. You see, most grocery stores track your purchases a lot more closely than you might think. The one I use the most started sending me coupons a few years ago for $4 off if I purchase $40 or more. Pretty good deal, right? Several months later, they started sending me the same coupon, but for $6 off when I spend $60 or more. I actually got up to an $8 off coupon when I spend $80 or more. I finally figured out the process. I was probably averaging $25 to $30 per week when the first coupon came out. Then, they got me to the next level and so on and so on. The grocery store, obviously, is always trying to get you to spend a little bit more money. And they know that if you walk in there with that coupon for a discount if you spend more than $60, and you normally only spend $50, then you will probably pick out $10 worth of stuff that you may or may not need. The key is to NEVER buy anything just because you have one of these coupons. Group your purchases (or stock up) on the items you buy most to meet their threshold.

Personally, I do not clip coupons the way that I could or the way that I should. First, I think it violates my Time/Work theory. The reason I say that is because the majority of what my household buys is fresh vegetables and fresh fish and chicken. That is about it along with the everyday staples of eggs, milk, butter, cheese, etc. So, I don't know that there are a lot of coupons out there for me to clip. I am sure I could save a lot more if I did, but I just don't. But there are substantial savings for those that do.

I do know a lot of people that do use coupons on a regular basis, and they will tell you things about the ability to use coupons that are already expired (most grocers do not care as far as I have heard), or also being able to use name brand coupons on similar items (your coupon is for Kraft shredded cheese, but you buy sliced cheese, or something like that). I will not advocate doing this, but I have heard that you can do it.

I also know that a lot of people who do use coupons on a consistent basis will also go out and buy a second Sunday paper to double their savings, if the first one they get has a great deal of coupon savings in it for them. There is absolutely nothing wrong with that.

If most of your grocery shopping is done through one particular grocer, they should be sending you so-called "customer appreciation" coupons in the mail. These are besides the generic ones that come with the Sunday paper. If they are not, stop by their customer service department and ask if there is a program or a mailing list you can sign up for.

With regards to clipping coupons out of the Sunday paper and out of all the flyers that you get in the mail—if you say you don't have the time to do it, it is like saying that you don't have time to save money. If it is worth doing. What I mean by that is, if the items that you buy the most are items that they have coupons for, then your savings should make it worth doing. An extra five minutes out of each day to go through the flyers you get in the mail, and then on Sundays an extra thirty minutes or so going through the paper should be well worth the savings that you can find. Look at it this way—this works out to be approximately one hour a week. If you can save around $15 per week, then it is probably worth your time, because more than likely this $15 that you just saved (oh, and it's also money you don't pay taxes on), is more than you make at your job.

I would definitely try it for a week and see what you can find. Maybe even involve the kids—make a game out of it. Tell them to try to find all of the foods that are eaten in your family in the newspaper and see how many coupons they can find.

The following are some other tips and pointers to make your "couponing" more successful:

–If the coupon says "on the purchase of two" you can usually get by with only purchasing one.

–Find a store that "doubles" your coupons and shop there!

–Take advantage of the "buy one get one free" items plus your coupons.

–Try to only buy things when they are on sale. Most stores run their sales in rotation so to speak—if it's not on sale this week, it is likely to be next week.

The only trap that I would try not to fall in is buying something just because you have a coupon for it. After all, that's the main goal by your grocer, isn't it? Only get it if it is something you normally buy or maybe something you would like to try out.

Stock up...

For items that are non-perishable or can fit in your freezer—when you see that they are on sale, stock up! Canned goods, fresh chicken, etc. That way, you NEVER have to pay full price for these items. This is another golden rule of shopping—NEVER PAY FULL PRICE WHEN YOU DON'T HAVE TO. Some people who are much more serious about grocery shopping than I am will tell you to never ever pay full price at all. I guess if you are organized enough and sharp enough you could come to this level. What I like to do is check the sale items because sometimes the grocer will list when the sale expires; that way I know how much time I have to utilize the savings.

This leads me to my infamous chicken story. Let me tell you about chicken. First of all, I would venture to say that every single household in America probably eats chicken and probably eats a fair amount of it. My household certainly does. We mostly buy the boneless skinless breasts, because any other kind of chicken that you want (strips, bites, etc.) you can cut yourself and save some money. In our household, we probably consume two of those packs a week. These are the packs that usually have about three fairly decent sized breasts in them. The packs usually weigh about two pounds. Let's say it weighs exactly two for argument's sake. When it is not on sale, it is generally about $6 per pound. About once every month, they put it on sale for $2 per pound, which is obviously the time to go and buy it. I usually try to keep eight packs in my freezer. We usually have enough room for this—and our freezer is small. I have never paid full price for chicken since I have become a smarter shopper and I never will. The math, and the savings, on this example alone are pretty mind-boggling. Let's go through it. We use two packs a week, which is eight packs a month. If I paid full price for it, I would be spending roughly $100 a month on chicken, and $1200 annually. Well, since I never pay full price for it and I am a smart shopper, I really only pay $32 per month, which is a little under $400 per year. How about that! If you were paying full price for your chicken, I just saved you $800 per year. That concept alone is worth far more than the price of this book!

Check flyers ...

Let's begin this section with an alert, and it is an alert that definitely applies to grocery shopping, but also applies to any kind of purchasing at all that you do.

Alert:

JUST BECAUSE IT'S ON SALE DOES NOT MEAN YOU CAN'T FIND IT SOMEWHERE ELSE FOR CHEAPER!

This is a good concept to begin learning. That is why I use more than one grocery store. I don't always check their Web sites for their weekly specials, but it might be a good idea to do this. I would suggest either doing this or checking the Sunday paper or your mailbox for your grocer's flyer. It is definitely worth your time.

Now that I use more than one grocery store, there is nothing more annoying than to walk into my second grocery store and see something on sale for a cheaper price than I just paid at my first store—all because I didn't read their flyer.

For example: One week, when I was doing my grocery shopping, I found blueberries that were supposedly on special at all four of the stores that I use. One store had a sign that said, "Blueberries, on special, $3.99" (this was the specialty store that I use). The second store's sign said, "Blueberries, two for $5." The third had them on special for two for $4, and finally, my farmer's market—which really has no advertised specials, no flyers, or anything, didn't even have any kind of special sign up. They just had the little price tag next to the blueberries for $1.89.

My point is, don't fall in love with the "on sale" sign—it doesn't necessarily mean that the price for that item is cheaper than anywhere else.

Generics...

I don't know your thoughts on it, but I am going to mention it. If you are serious about saving money, or serious about getting out of debt, I would seriously consider buying store brands or generic brands of food, at least on a temporary basis. Most stores now offer their own version or a cheaper version of just about everything out there. I have another news flash for you—the difference in taste is minimal. Again, make it into a thirty-day trial if you want to, but I guarantee you that you can make an impact on your wallet if you switch to these brands, at least in the short term.

Open your eyes...

Pay attention to sales. Like I said before, it makes sense to at least browse through the weekly flyer of the stores around you; you never know what you might find. But also, pay attention to sales in general. Sometimes, grocery stores will put a price tag so low on something that it is just too good to pass up. I wouldn't fall into this trap of picking up this stuff every week; it is just a good idea to keep your eyes open.

You see, I do the majority of the grocery shopping in my family. If I had my way, I would get it all done in less than an hour. Actually, if it could take me five minutes that would be great. I have a very young son at home whom I love very much, and every minute that I can spend with him is very precious to me. Therefore, most of the time, I am like an Indy car racer going through the grocery store with my shopping cart. I generally know exactly what I want, I get it as fast as I can, I pay for it as fast as I can, and I'm gone. Well, there have been a few times where I have actually stopped to look a little bit at the things around me, and guess what, I found out and figured out more ways to save money. First, sometimes you will find sales on items that are just too good to pass up. Maybe it is for an item that you use to cook something that you eat, but you don't eat it very often. Well, if they have a rock-bottom price on it, and it is non-perishable, pick up a few. That way, you won't have to worry about it the next time you want to make that dish.

Here is another thing that recently dawned on me. At my grocery store, I try to buy the store brand or generic brand of many of the items that we use on a consistent basis. For obvious reasons—because they are always cheaper. There are some things that I use and some things that my wife uses where a particular brand name is either needed or highly preferred. Take deodorant, for example. There is a specific brand that I use, and I use it because I like it and I have used it for a long time (it also just so happens to be one of the cheaper ones). However, this is my point. There are these few things where a specific brand name is either needed or desired, but think of all the other items that you use where you don't care what the brand name is. Maybe you don't care but you still buy the same brand all the time. For me, a good example would be laundry detergent. I do not use a generic or store brand name, but besides that, I could care less which kind it is. I could care less, but I usually pick out the same brand. Well, in these instances it is a good idea to check out all the other prices in the section where that laundry detergent is. Because invariably, somebody always has their laundry detergent on sale at a price cheaper than the one you buy, and you don't even care that you buy that brand. Keep your eyes open for all of these items, spend an extra two minutes in that aisle and pick out the cheapest one.

I could probably write an entire book on the art of grocery shopping, because I truly believe that it is an art. I only hope I can remember all of the tips and habits that have I come up with over the years that allow me to save as much as I do on my groceries. Remember, more than likely, it is the second biggest expense in your household, so the opportunities for savings, and the opportunities for impacting your overall personal economy are many.

Research Your Purchases

I would now like to get into probably the most important section in this chapter. It kind of draws on most of the different concepts that I have practiced over the past several years. It basically involves the purchase of any other item besides your groceries. Let's say any other item that costs more than $30. I want to emphasis to you again that I have not become so fanatical about saving pennies that I would apply these concepts to when you want to buy a pack of gum, but for me, I usually put the cut off around $30.

Let's begin by re-emphasizing the alert that I put in the last chapter because it applies to normal purchases as well. Just because something is on sale somewhere does not mean you cannot find it somewhere else for cheaper.

For this particular example, a portable DVD player would be good, and obviously your savings will increase the more expensive the item is—all the way up to home furniture, a home computer, or even a new car. The key here is RESEARCH. We'll use the DVD player as an example. Most of us do not wake up one morning and decide right at that moment that we will buy ourselves a portable DVD player and we proceed directly to the nearest store and buy it at that moment. We have at least thought about it for a few days. Now, if I were buying a new portable DVD player for myself, this is the exact process I would go through. I would start a generic search on the internet to determine (or narrow down) which brand I wanted, with which features, and one that was in my price range. Then, I would do a search on that particular brand. If I couldn't find the cheapest price through an online outlet (don't forget to factor in the shipping costs you'll pay) then, I would probably go to all of the three major appliance outlets that I have in my area (all within five to ten miles) to see if they had a comparable one with my benefits and features at a cheaper price, also checking out any other specials on portable DVD players they might have. Maybe I could forego a feature or two to save some money, maybe I could get a few extra features for the original price I was willing to spend. I would make my final decision and make my purchase.

All in all, I could not have spent THAT much extra time, and I know I would have gotten what I wanted for the cheapest price possible. Your savings here are all relative depending on the cost of the item, and there is more to this whole process, but I think you understand the basics. Also, I would imagine most of you did not know that for higher end items that you can actually negotiate the price down depending on where you are buying from. Let me explain.

You have to understand that these people want to sell you the item as much as you want to buy the item, and you would be surprised at the number of times you can get something for a cheaper price, just by asking the person you're dealing with if they can do any better on the price. If they say no, fine, but it never hurts to ask. You may have thought that there was a more involved explanation coming, but that is really it. Just ask them. Tell them you don't have enough money for the price on the item, tell them that their price is $50 higher than your budget for the item, tell them anything you can think of. If they knock off an extra $20 just because you asked, that's another $20 saved.

The process that I just laid out for you does seem like it is fairly time consuming when looked at objectively. But, I am sure you remember the premium that I place on my time, so if you do this right, it really won't take you any extra time at all.

That is because I do not get up one morning and go to one store and then to the next and then to the next. I have already thought about this DVD player for a few days, and I just keep it in the back of my head that the next time I go to one of these stores where I want to research the item, that I need to check out the DVD players. So, I just factor it into my daily routine and it really doesn't take me any extra time at all.

Another thing that going through this process does for you is that it confirms for you that you really want the item. This was one of my concepts in Chapter 2 (*Do you really need it?*). If you go through this process, sometimes you'll find out that you don't really need the item you're thinking about purchasing, or you'll also find out from time to time that you don't really WANT the item.

Everything Else

Here is a section with everything else I can think of that I do to spend less money in my daily life.

My car. I am not embarrassed to say that I currently am driving a 1994 Toyota Tercel, and we are in October of 2009. So, yes, the car is fifteen years old. It has just over 139,000 miles on it, which I will elaborate on in a minute. Now, am I advocating that everyone drive a car around for fifteen years? Absolutely not. I had actually planned on getting rid of this car several years ago, but other things kept coming up to where I decided it made more sense to keep it for the time being. I was investing in my wife's business, improvements came up that I wanted to do on my house, etc.

What am trying to say is that first of all, you may want to consider driving the car you are currently driving for just a few more years. It is hard for me to understand, but I know quite a few people out there that "need" to have a new car every four years, or even every three years, or even every other year! Well, that's fine if you can comfortably afford it. But keep in mind that there are a lot of extra expenses that you generate by doing this in your life. Well, maybe not actual expenses, but you are forfeiting quite a few substantial savings by continuing this habit. Again, I am not saying that you need to drive your current car for the next twenty years, but you may consider stretching out your timetable just a little until you get your personal economy jump-started.

First, you will always have to come up with this down payment every few years. This is money that could definitely be spent better elsewhere. And, if you are not coming up with a substantial down payment each time you get a new car, more than likely, you are paying a higher interest rate for the loan on your car.

You also have to deal with being in the unenviable position of being "upside-down" in your car. What is "upside-down?" Well, that means that you owe more on your car than it's worth. Generally, this occurs for the first few years after you buy a brand-new car. Obviously, once your car is paid off, then you are never upside-down, but I think we all know that a brand-new car loses a lot of its value the second it is driven off of the lot. This may not seem like a big deal, but if you wreck your car six months after owning it, you could be in for some long financial times ahead paying off the loan on it.

And finally, I'd like to mention life without a car payment. This seemed like such a dream for me for so long. The last two cars that I drove before my current one were both "totaled" just a few months before being paid off. No lie. One accident was my fault, the other one wasn't. So after spending virtually my entire adult life with a monthly car payment, I finally reached this grand state of being sometime around 1999. It still feels good to this day. Having that extra $250 or so really helps out a lot, and I guess in the back of my mind this is another reason why I am still driving my classic!

Eating out. I'd like to mention one of the most favorite pastimes for Americans, and that is eating out. I enjoy eating out as much as anybody, but I also learned to forego this luxury while I was digging myself out of my hole. Just about any way you look at it, eating out is expensive, or, at the very least, more expensive than eating in. Food prepared at home is much cheaper than in a restaurant no matter what.

If you really enjoy eating out so much that you can't envision giving it up or even making it into a thirty-day trial, at least try adopt these tips into your eating out schedule.

Coupons— You can always find tons of coupons for new and even existing restaurants. They are worth looking into and definitely worth using. Plus, if you like to try out new restaurants or ones that you've never been to before, you should definitely be able to find a coupon for your particular restaurant. Also, during these tough economic times, restaurants have also been hit particularly hard and are doing anything to drum up business. You may be able to find a coupon for your favorite restaurant even though they may have never "coupon-ed" before.

Limit alcohol—the amount of money that a restaurant makes off of alcohol is much higher than what it makes off of food. I would suggest either drinking your cocktails at home before you leave, or at least limiting the amount of alcohol you order at the restaurant. And for your beverages in general, I would always order water. This helps keep down the total amount of the bill.

Skip/split dessert—this is the same as for alcohol. Restaurants make lots of money off of desserts. Why do I tell you this? I tell you this about alcohol and desserts because it means you can save substantially more money by limiting/eliminating these things from your dining experience. Skip the dessert and stop off at your local ice cream spot and get a cone. Or stick some ice cream in your freezer at home and really save!

Garbage—This one may be the oddest bits of advice I give in this whole book, and some may find it a little distasteful, but, it works for me and it has saved me a pretty good chunk of change over the years. I want to talk to you about garbage. You see, I was born and raised in Ohio, and when I was a child, we just dragged our garbage out to the side of the road and they came and got it once a week. Then, when I was about sixteen, my family moved to Florida. When we were first settling in, we had so many other things going on that we just assumed garbage pickup worked the same way. So we asked a neighbor what day garbage day was, and on that day, we dragged our garbage out to the street and hoped they'd come pick it up. Well, that "garbage day" passed and our garbage was still there. OK, we thought, maybe it was because no one has lived in this house for a while and they missed it. The next day went by and no garbage pickup. It wasn't until the following day when some sympathetic neighbor knocked on our door and asked us if we actually signed up for garbage service. Sign up? Why would we have to sign up? Well, came the great answer, because it costs money.

My parents really didn't have much of a choice, so they called and signed up and have paid for garbage pickup ever since. Well, simply put, not me. I had been through my entire childhood with free garbage pickup and I just never really could digest the fact of having to pay extra for it. And yes, I would consider it to be paying "extra." The reason I say this is that somewhere between the sales tax that I pay whenever I buy anything, to the property taxes that I pay on my home, to the state and federal income taxes that I pay every year, there has got to be some money in there to pay the sanitary engineers.

Without any grand statement about unfair taxation or anything like that, I simply decided that I was not going to pay for garbage pickup. Ever. And here is my solution. It worked quite well for me when I worked in the restaurant business because we always had a dumpster located close to the building, but I would imagine that this advice could be applied to anyone that has a job. And, even if you didn't have a job, I am sure you could find a way to make it work.

In my house, I have several small garbage cans in my different rooms. I think I have one in the kitchen, one in both bathrooms, and one in my computer room. Every morning before I leave for work, I simply gather the bags from the kitchen and any others that may be full, toss them in my trunk (and no, my trunk does not smell like garbage, not at all), and I simply toss this stuff into my dumpster at work each morning. It takes me about three seconds each morning.

I think the benefits are numerous. First, I never ever have full garbage cans of trash inside my house; second, I don't have some huge smelly trash can filling up in back of my house, which is what I would have if I paid for service. If anything, I think it makes both my house and my property cleaner, and even more trash-free. There is also the cost benefit. The last time I checked I think it cost around $50 every three months to pay for trash pickup. I am quite sure this has gone up considerably, but even with that modest number, I have saved right around $1800 since I have lived in my current home. That is close to four house payments for me! After reading that number, I bet you stopped laughing at what you probably thought was the silliest idea in this book.

And also, if you recycle your paper, plastic and glass, then you will find that you probably do not generate as much garbage as you may have originally thought.

Learn to cook and use use fresh– These are basically tied together. First of all, I would suggest learning to cook if you or someone in your household does not currently know how to. Granted, it is hard for me to speak objectively on this subject, because cooking has always been a passion of mine. I have loved to cook since I was a child. But the benefits of doing your own cooking are many. First, you will save a lot of money. Buying fresh is almost always more financially sound than buying processed or already prepared. I would say that approximately seventy percent of our groceries come from the farmers' market. Second, learning to cook is fun. At least I think so. It allows you to utilize any creativity you may have swimming around in your head, and also allows you to eat the dishes you really want to eat. Third, it is much healthier than eating foods out of packages. There is no question about this. And finally, food just tastes much better when it is prepared fresh. I could go on forever about this subject since it is a passion of mine, but I will leave it at that. Find some way to learn how to cook if someone in your household currently does not, and try to increase the amounts of food that you eat that are freshly prepared. It will take a little bit more of your time, but the benefits are well worth your efforts.

Along with this, if you have already begun to cook or are in the process, try to use "fresh" as much as possible. I will put this to you in as simple as terms as I can. You will find very little food in my freezer at any point in time. About the only thing in there besides ice cream and things like that are fresh chicken and fish that I will use in the future, and every once in a while I will buy a bag of frozen cut vegetables. These are quite handy when you are in hurry and I think I've even seen research that shows that the nutritional content in them is close to that of fresh veggies. They are cheap and the taste is quite similar.

Besides that, it is fresh all the way. This can really increase your savings if you are able to find a local farmers' market in your area. I am always amazed at the prices that I see for veggies at my regular grocer compared to what I get them for at the market. It has probably subconsciously spurred me on to buy even more. And again, of course it is much healthier for you.

Brown-bag it– I want to talk to you about something else that can save you another big chunk of change if you commit to it– "brown-bagging" it, or preparing your own lunch and taking it to work with you. This may not seem like much savings, but hear me out.

I worked in the restaurant business for a long time, so at that point in my life, brown-bagging was not needed in my life. I always ate for free. When I entered the professional world outside of restaurants, it seemed to me that most people ate out for lunch and ate out every single day. First, I never saw the sense in this because although I enjoy eating out, I enjoy home-cooked meals even more. Second, I love to cook, so preparing my own lunch was never a problem. And of course, I would be lying if I did not say that I thought it was a waste of money.

Depending on what I decide to take for my lunch, it might take three minutes out of my day. Most of the time, it simply involves filling a leftover container with something we had for dinner the night before. Sometimes I prepare sandwiches or something, and of course I try to change it up as much as possible, but the savings are huge and you are eating fresh instead of pre-processed restaurant food. If you currently take your lunch at a restaurant that actually prepares its food as close to home-cooked as possible, then more power to you. However, most employees at my place of work seem to still gravitate to the old-time favorite for lunch—fast food.

For the economic benefit, let's lay out this example. Let's say it costs you $5 a lunch for five days a week (which is an incredibly conservative estimate). Now let's say it costs you $1 to bring your own. (If you ever decided to cost out your leftovers, or whatever it is you might be taking with you for lunch, you'll probably find that this is not too far off the mark). That means if you started to "brown-bag" it, you would save $80 in the first month alone, and close to $1,000 in your first year. That is a pretty impressive number! And we are not even taking into account the amount of gas you would save from not having to drive to a restaurant every day. Let's conservatively say that you save 50 cents per day in gas. You can now add another $120 to your yearly savings.

And a final note. When I first entered the non-restaurant business world and decided to brown-bag it, one thing that concerned me a little was how I would look to my co-workers. Would there be snickers? Would they talk about me behind my back?? Would I be called cheap?

I mention this mostly in jest because first of all, I could care less what others think about me. However, I did think about it a little, but guess what? The opposite turned out to be true. Whenever I was asked about why I "brown-bagged," I just said I was trying to save money and I like preparing my own lunch. After that, it was like there was this newfound respect for me, rather than being the subject of jokes. So, if that is one of your concerns, you should forget about it.

Consolidate Driving Trips—Another thing that you can do that will save you money is to consolidate your driving trips. It is hard to assign a dollar value to your savings (probably nearly impossible); however, it works for you on two different fronts. First, you save gas which saves money; second, you save time. These, to me, are the two most valuable assets in my life (besides my family).

The best way to do it is to simply see if you can re-organize your schedule to where you do more while you are out, and to eliminate trips where you leave your house for just one thing. Obviously, you cannot do this completely, and there are always things that come up for me at the last minute, and there's nothing I can do about it. But maybe you can do your weekly trip to the grocery store(s) on your way home from work, rather than a separate trip out. Maybe on your off day, you can knock out the bank, the dry cleaners, and filling your tank all at the same time. Everyone's daily routine is different so unfortunately you'll have to do the legwork here yourself. But it will save you gas and it will save you time. A win/win.

Dollar store shopping—OK, OK, I think I can already hear the groans. If any of you have ever been in a dollar store before, you're probably groaning. You walk in, and it looks like one of your children's bedrooms. The shelves haven't been restocked in a few days, and it looks like kids have terrorized the items that are on the shelves. Nothing is organized, nothing is labeled. It is difficult to find anything. And then, when you do find your items, it could take up to a few days to actually check out, depending on how long it takes an employee to stroll over to the cash register to ring you up. Or, if by some miracle, there is some sole employee already stationed there, there are probably six other people in line waiting to check out.

Such has been my experience with dollar stores in general. No offense meant to the employees or operators of these stores, it has just been my general experience and impression of them. However, having said all that, you can save quite a bit of money at these places.

First, I would relate back to my section on grocery shopping about things where you could care less of the brand name. These are perfect items to pick up at the dollar store. Dishwashing liquid or detergent, laundry detergent, and general cleaning supplies are usually consistently cheaper here.

Also, on another note, let's talk about toys for kids. My son loves toys, and he wants a new toy every time we go to a store together. Most of the time, he could really care less what it is, he just wants something new. Well, here is another perfect opportunity to utilize the dollar store. Everything's a dollar, remember? I have purchased quite a few toys for my son there. Which works out well considering his attention span for these toys could be as short as two minutes at times. So it really helps out my wallet, and my stress level, when I know that what he is tossing into his basket after only a few seconds of playing only set me back a buck.

There is one thing to watch out for at these dollar stores, though. Try to take a look at the quality of what you're buying with respect to cleaning supplies. Of course, detergents and what not should have the same quality, but you can probably count on towels having less of a shelf life before they start to fall apart, and other things like this. Also, keep in mind that these dollar stores do sell lots of items (at a dollar) that you might think you're getting a deal on, when actually you can get them for less than a dollar at your local grocer. So don't just haphazardly go in there and fill up a grocery cart full of stuff thinking that every single thing on their shelves is cheaper than anywhere else, because you would be wrong. It probably won't happen a lot, but you have to pay attention to what you are buying.

Turn off lights/appliances—Here is a simple one, but I question how often people actually follow it. How about turning off a light when you leave a room, or turning off the TV or any other appliance when no one is watching it, using it, or listening to it. This habit was ingrained into me when I was very young, and it is now almost irritating when I see an empty room lit up in my house. I cannot imagine that it would take very long at all to put this habit into your life, and guess what? It involves absolutely no sacrifice—you're not giving anything up at all. It simply involves a little common sense. I doubt there is a dollar amount to these savings either, but obviously, you are saving money. I have actually heard that some people out there even take the extra step of unplugging devices that aren't in use, as they say that even something that is not turned on is still using energy simply by being plugged in. I will be completely honest with you by saying that I have never done this and doubt I would ever consider doing this because of the inconvenience, but I know that some people have taken into this level.

Run appliances at night— This mainly goes for your dishwasher and your washer/dryer. I know it may not be possible to do your washer/dryer at night because of your schedule, but the dishwasher should be doable. I do the washer/dryer thing probably half the time but I do the dishwasher almost exclusively at night. This is because these items obviously give off heat, so in the summertime, you are keeping your house from warming up even more during the day, and in the winter time you are helping to keep your house warm at night. These keep the AC from working as hard during the summer time and your heater from working as hard in the winter time.

Also, there is a good chance that you pay more for your electricity during the day then you do at night. Can you imagine that? If your electricity meter is digital, rather than the old-fashioned type with dials, then this is especially true. Electricity rates are some times as much as three times higher during the day than they are after ten o'clock at night.

Pay your bills online—I know that some of you out there may still be a little leery of the internet and your personal information, but I can assure you that I have never had any issues. It took me a little while to take the plunge and do my banking online, but I was sure glad I did after I finally decided to do it.

The benefits to online banking are many. First, it is much easier and more convenient to pay your bills online. Of course, I still keep a balanced checkbook and I would suggest you do the same, because mistakes are always possible. However, besides the convenience factor, there are ways that online banking saves you money as well. First, you eliminate the need (for the most part) for stamps in your life. Think about it. I would guess that the average person has approximately ten bills to pay every month. Well, currently, stamps are going for 44 cents apiece. That's $4.40 per month that you are saving, which translates into just over $50 per year. Hey, fifty bucks is fifty bucks.

Second, your check usage decreases considerably which means you won't have to order checks as often.

I guess that's really it from a savings standpoint but it also saves you another precious commodity—time. If you organize it correctly and stick with it, you can turn your bill paying process into about a ten- to fifteen-minute system on a monthly basis. And I know that would take up less time than writing out ten checks per month.

As far as I can tell, that is absolutely positively every single way that I save more money in my everyday life. That is of course, until I come up with the next way. These ideas don't come nearly quite as often as they used to, but I have put into place two or three of the ideas that you are reading here in this book during the actual writing of it!

CHAPTER 4

Spending Less

"The art is not in making money, but keeping it." - Proverb

Now, I guess when it comes right down to it, the "saving more" and "spending less" chapters could really be interchangeable, because it's all really the same thing. But then again, is it? Well, this is the way that I look at it. There are actually two ways to keep more money in your wallet. The first is to simply leave it in your wallet in the first place, and the second is to take as less out of it as possible. I guess it may be considered splitting hairs, but to me, there is a difference. And coming from the situation that I was in, anything I could do to help was something that I was willing to try. You could probably relate this to the "emptying the tub" analogy I used earlier. I guess here, your goal is to "fill the tub" and the two ways to do that are, by putting more water in from the faucet, and by fixing any leaks that are in the bottom of the tub. Well, I guess the point of this chapter is fixing the leaks.

So, let's continue with some ways to keep more of your money in your wallet. And again, though you may be getting tired of hearing it, some of these things involve more of a change in mindset rather than a concrete A, B, C type list of things to do.

Eliminate the "why nots." OK, when you go to a convenience store, I would imagine that ninety percent of the time, your original reason for going there is to put gas in your car. Try to keep it that way. If that's all you are there for, then just buy the gas. Did you know that these convenience stores actually make very little money off of the gas they sell you? It's everything else you buy where they make their profits. Because they charge you substantially more than what you would pay for the same item in another store. Do you get a cup of coffee every morning when you fill up?? Invest in a coffee maker and make it at home. Always stopping to get a Coke? First, that stuff is not very good for your insides and second, if you have to have it, buy a twelve-pack from your grocery store and take it from home. I could give a similar scenario for virtually everything else purchased at a convenience store.

This involves a change in mindset and this would be a perfect opportunity to try your first "thirty-day trial" if you have not already. As a matter of fact, I think it was my first. I used to be like a kid in a candy store going into those convenience stores. Of course, the real reason was only to get gas, but by the time I was done, I had a newspaper, some sort of candy or snack, a Coke, maybe a lottery ticket or two, some cigarettes, and maybe some beer for the evening. It was insane. I have already addressed most of what I just mentioned, but here's what you do with the rest—lottery tickets (just stop because the odds are stacked against you. I mean, REALLY, just stop). Cigarettes (you should just stop, but if not possible, at least in the beginning, consider buying a carton to save some money). Beer (again, maybe cut back on this, but if not possible, go to a liquor store—it is much cheaper). I think you get my point. Most spending can simply be eliminated, and all of it can be reduced.

Do it yourself. When I first began my quest to save as much money as I possibly could in every possible way, my mechanical abilities included all of maybe knowing how to hook up a DVD player and I could recognize a screwdriver from a hammer. So I know that ANY of you guys could at least learn what I've learned. This goes for women, too, but for those of you girls that can't, find a guy somewhere in your life and I am sure he can. Become, at least to some extent, a Do-it-Yourself-er. You can find out how to do ANYTHING around your home or in your car (as long as it's not too major) either on the Internet or by asking the experts at your local Home Depot or hardware store. They are experts and nine time out of ten they know what they're talking about. For example, toilet workings, kitchen faucet, air filters, minor electrical work, closet shelving, landscaping, minor car repairs (oil changes, spark plugs), etc. Plus, when all is said and done, you'll look a lot cooler in front of the women, if that matters.

Bills. For most of us, I would imagine that most of our utility bills come in the regular mail to us, and we simply look at the amount due and write out the check for that amount due and send it in before the due date. Well, there is nothing really wrong with that process, except for one key thing: *Checking your bills for accuracy.* A long time ago, this never really occurred to me and I simply blindly sent in my payment. I mean, how could these companies ever make a mistake? Well, believe it or not, it can happen. And believe it or not, if the error is in your favor, ninety-nine percent of the time, they will find it; however, when the error benefits them, they will conveniently overlook it. I know that must be shocking to hear, but it is true.

I will get into exactly how to handle these bill discrepancies at the end of the chapter. For now, let's go through some ways that you can spend less on your actual bills.

Your mortgage (or rent). For those of you that own a home, there are two key ways you can impact your monthly house payment. First, and this might be a no-brainer, can you re-finance? With the housing market the way it is these days, it is DEFINITELY worth looking into, even if you re-financed recently in the past. You want to look into it with a trustworthy mortgage person (very important to have one of these in your life, but more on that later). You can get ripped off if you're not careful. You need to make sure that you can absorb any closing costs within about three years of doing so (meaning, the amount you save should offset the closing costs in less than three years), and you should not be paying any points or added fees (besides closing), but again, you need to get with a mortgage person you can trust. For those of you that rent, ever thought about moving? You don't think there are renters out there that are dying for your business (or tenancy)? Take advantage of the slow economy. Break out the apartment finder guide, or there is probably a business dedicated to this service in your area. If you could save $100 month and still live in a decent place, don't you think it's worth looking into? Remember, that $100 per month translates into $1200 per year.

Also, for those of us who may have bought a new home for the first time in the last several years, if you have been paying down your principle at a fairly decent clip, there is something else that I want you to look into. You probably have a line on your mortgage statement that says something about PMI. PMI stands for Private Mortgage Insurance, and lenders require it for anyone who purchases a home with less than twenty percent of the value of the home as a down payment. However, when you reach twenty percent equity in your house, PMI is no longer necessary and can be taken off of your mortgage. This level can be reached by appreciation in your house, improvements made to your house, or simply by paying down on your mortgage.

At the very least, if you are still required to pay PMI as part of your mortgage, make your lender calculate roughly when you should no longer have to pay it so you won't forget to call them to take it off of your mortgage. This can be a savings of between $25 and $100 per month and could save you thousands over the life of your mortgage.

Heating/electric—About four or five years ago, when I was still trying to get back on my financial feet, I kept my house at seventy-two degrees in the summer and seventy-six degrees in the winter. Sound about right to you? Well after I decided to pare down my bills wherever I could, I played a little game with my thermostat. The first year, I moved it to seventy-three in the summer and seventy-five in the winter. After a few days or so, I never noticed the difference. Time went on, and I kept playing the game…and do you know where my thermostat is now??? Seventy-eight in the summer and sixty-nine in the winter. One thing you have to remember is that these changes do not have to be permanent, so even if it is a sacrifice for you, just tell yourself that it's not forever, and pretty soon you should be OK with it, especially after you see the savings (revisit section on thirty-day trials). Each degree you move your thermostat should save you around five percent on your heating bill. For me, that was probably more than $100 per year. Another quick point—that's how you need to look at all of these savings measures—on a yearly basis. This is my "times twelve rule" in play again. If you get your first AC bill and it is a whopping $9 lower because of your changes, you are liable to think it's not worth it and give up. ALWAYS multiply that by twelve and you are more likely to stick with it.

Also, one thing that I always wondered about was how could one save *more* money on one's power bill— by turning your AC off completely while at work, and letting the entire house cool down at night when you return home, or simply turning your thermostat "up" during the day, to make for less of a cool-down in the evening. In the first instance, your unit is not running the entire day, but it is working harder in the evening to cool down the entire house, and to cool down a warmer house so to speak. In the second example, your AC would run from time to time throughout the day, but would require less work to cool down the house in the evening.

What I found out is that it is more energy efficient to turn off the AC completely while you're gone rather than simply turning it up. Obviously, this only applies to those of us who have empty houses during the day. And this is why.

Simply put, heat goes to where it isn't. When your AC is turned off completely, your house absorbs heat from outside, but at some point it will be so hot it can't absorb any more heat. So when you come home and turn the AC on, the AC has to remove this heat only one time. This is where the savings comes in, even though your AC unit will be working a little bit harder to take all of that heat out of your house.

If the AC is on when you're gone, then your house is constantly absorbing heat because your AC is constantly cooling down the house. Your AC is removing absorbed heat over and over again.

Let's say you leave the AC off, and your house absorbs 20k BTUs of heat and then stops, because that's all it can absorb. When you come home at night, your AC will remove these 20k BTUs one time and one time only.

Now let's say that you have the AC running instead. The house absorbs 5k BTUs of heat, so the AC turns on. Then it absorbs another 5k BTUs and your AC turns on again. And again and again and again. So, it is fairly simple and elementary—turning your AC off in the a.m. and turning it back on at night will save you more money in the long run.

Now, maybe you don't want to actually go through doing this at night—I mean, who wants to come home to a "hot" house? Well, this is how I would look at it. First of all, now you know what to do if you ever go on vacation during the summer—definitely turn that air off instead of just turning it up. Second, as far as doing it on a daily basis during the summer, why not try it at first to see how "awful" it really is. When

I first started doing it, I thought it would be unbearable. But guess what, I realized that when I come home from work at night, it is not like I walk in and immediately go to the couch and sit down and realize the house is too hot and I hate it and why am I trying to save these stupid pennies in the first place. Actually, I found that when I come home, I am still doing some so-called little "chores" before I am actually sitting down to relax. Opening the mail, turning on the TV, getting something ready for supper, etc. What I found was that by the time I was ready to actually sit down and relax, the house was either already at a comfortable level or it was real close. And another thing that I found was that during the summer when it is hot out, the first thing I like to do when I do arrive home from work is to take a shower. Well, if you're going to be under the cool water for the first ten minutes of arriving home anyways, who needs a cool house for that? In the end, it all worked out and I was able to save money, and pretty soon after I turned it into a habit and I never even noticed it at all.

Cable—I would assume most of you have television through a cable company or satellite company. If that is the case, I would ask you to look at the following things—if you are paying for a subscription movie service like HBO, Showtime, etc., or if you have one of those sports packages like NFL Sunday Ticket, I want you to think about whether you really need these or not. I can tell you this much—I don't pay for a movie service, but even when my cable company advertises something like a free Showtime weekend, I don't even watch movies then. And with the sports thing, how can you really watch eight football games at one time anyways? Again, it is not about giving up this stuff forever, but rather a temporary thing until you can get closer to where you want to be financially (once again, if Showtime costs

$15 per month and you give it up for one year, you are saving yourself $180).

Phone bill—As you can see, we are moving down the list from bills you can probably save the most on, to ones not as much, but depending on how much you pay for local telephone service, this one could actually add up to some good savings. If you have a cell phone, the best advice I can give you about your local telephone service is to…GET RID OF IT. What do you need it for? Need it for an Internet connection? I would consider upgrading to Internet where a landline isn't needed. I can think of no other reason to keep a landline in your home. Either do without, or if you do need a line coming out of your home, look into Magic Jack, Vonage, or any of the other companies out there. They are VOIPs (Voice over Internet Providers) where you can get a phone line that is basically run through your computer. Check out all the details first, but I switched to Magic Jack several months ago, and I don't even notice a difference (except for far fewer annoying phone calls from telemarketers while I am trying to enjoy my dinner). There is a chance you may need to bump up the minutes on your cell phone plan, but you'll still save money in the long run. I had a bare-bones local phone plan when I switched, so when I made that move I saved only about $300 annually, but again, if for example, you pay $40 per month for your local service, you'll save just under $500 a year.

Water bill—Last but not least, your water bill. Save money on your water bill? How's that possible? Well, let me tell you—in a lot of ways. First and foremost, consider taking shorter showers. Now, this one in particular is tough to track, and again, you don't need to make all of these sacrifices forever, but just consider it. You can save about twenty gallons of water per shower. Second, consider turning the water off while you soap up (did you ever realize that it's actually easier to do this?) and finally, definitely, turn the water off while you are actually brushing your teeth or actually shaving. That water is just running down the drain. Back when I lived alone, I had my water bill down to a little over $14 per month. No lie. Nobody that I told ever believed me until I brought them my bill. It used to be about $14 per month.

Another thing about your water bill is that if you have a drippy water faucet, instead of just pretending like that annoying little noise isn't there, you should really fix it. A drippy faucet can waste up to 400 gallons of water per year, and if the water that is dripping is hot, you're losing the money to heat that water too. See my section on "Do-It-Yourself" and fix that sucker!

Another thing to do is to make sure you utilize your rinse cycle when washing clothes. It has been found that "rinsed" clothes require less water to wash than un-rinsed clothes.

Buying gasoline. Depending on how far your commute is to work, your monthly expense for gasoline could be fairly high up there on your list. Do you know what a discrepancy there is in the price of gas at the gas stations right in your local area? It never occurred to me until the price of gas went through the roof and I decided to check it out. I basically have an average commute to work—it's about eighteen to twenty miles. However, on my way to work, there are about ten gas stations. So, I looked at the price of gas at each station on my way to work. The first thing that I found out was that the difference between the cheapest and most expensive gas was more than 15 cents! I would stay away from using gas from a mom-and-pop convenience store, because the quality of the gas might not be that good. But, other than that, why not go with the cheapest? With my commute and the current price of gas, I spend about $200 per month in gas. When I started buying gas from the least expensive place on my way to work, I started saving about $150 per year. Obviously, for longer commutes, the savings will be bigger.

What else do I do in my daily life now to spend less?

Well, here is as good of a place as any to go over a very abstract concept that I use on a daily basis to do all of the three major things that I talk about in this book. It is what I do to save more, to spend less, and to generate more income in my life. I like to call it "thinking." Yup, it's as simple as that: **THINKING!**

The reason why I have been able to come up with ways to impact my personal economy in virtually every area of my life has come from nothing more than simply thinking about it. I do not think that I am obsessed with saving money, that it dominates my life, or that I am enjoying life any less because of the time that I am thinking about ways to save money. To the contrary. I think that I am living a happier life because I have more of the money that I earn to do the things that I want to do with it.

Let's just simply start to think about ways to save money. You remember my crazy idea about how to save money on your garbage? Here is another one. One day I was taking out my trash, and there is really not much on my mind when I am taking out the trash, and I decided to think for a second if there was any other way that I could save money in this area. Guess what—I realized that if I used the million plastic bags that I get from the grocery store in my garbage cans around the house, then I won't ever have to spend money on little garbage bags again. How do you think I came up with this idea? By just thinking about it.

Another example. One day, by mistake I loaded some computer paper that already had printing on it back into my printer instead of throwing it away. Instead of getting mad about having to re-print all of my stuff, I realized that for the stuff that I print that is not really important (which is what, about sixty percent of what we print?), if I simply turn my printer paper over and use the other side before I throw it away, then I can cut my cost of printer paper in half.

And finally, one day while I was standing in front of the mirror brushing my teeth, I looked down and saw all that water just running down the drain and I realized that there is no real reason to have the water running while I am actually brushing my teeth. Another little way to save some money.

So, try to actually start thinking about some of the things that you do on a daily basis, and if there might be a way to save some money while doing them. I bet you can probably come up with a variety of ways that I haven't even thought of yet!

Also, I always check my utility bills and especially my credit card bills. You would be surprised, but sometimes your utility companies will make a mistake on your bill. If the mistake is in your favor, they almost always find it and take it away. When the mistake is in their favor, usually, they will never do anything about it. Now, that statement may not be one hundred percent true, but it is a good mindset to have whether it is true or not. That way, you'll never lose out. I recently found a $100 mistake (not in my favor) on my electric bill. It did take a little while to get fixed, but I got it fixed. As far as credit card bills go, they usually don't make mistakes, but sometimes they do. I check mine every month more to make sure no one has stolen my identity than anything else. Additionally, most times you won't find any actual mistakes on your credit card bills, but you will find charges that either don't belong there or are incorrect.

Now, what you need to do when you find these mistakes can be tricky. If you're lucky, you simply call your utility company or credit card company, explain to them the error, and they fix it. Oh, but that would be if we lived in a perfect world. Most of the time, it does not go that easily. Most of the time, you will get told that there is no mistake, that if there is a mistake it is not their fault, that yes there was a mistake but you don't have enough proof for it, that if only you could tell them the name of the person you spoke with the last time you called they could help you out, and/or about a million other excuses.

So what follows is a pretty lengthy section on how to handle all of these things as they arise. One of the first things you need to realize is that this is YOUR money you are fighting for, so, you have to act that way. My ability to win these types of disputes has probably saved me as much money as all the other stuff in this book put together. That is probably exaggerated a little, but this section is well worth reading, and probably one of the most important ones in the book.

Disputes—

This section is actually quite lengthy, but that is for a very good reason. This is easily the single most "Don't Be A Mule" part of the entire book. I think every single one of us has come across a billing error on a utility bill, a charge that didn't belong on their credit card, or a company that did not treat them fairly or tried to charge them for something they really didn't think they should pay for. I think it's happened to all of us. After I got serious about my money, I also got very serious about how to deal with these situations. It is an art, and it is an acquired art, but the faster you learn how to not get "run over" in these types of situations the better off you'll be. Plus, I have saved myself a TON of money over the years by simply fighting back. And, not to sound arrogant, but I have yet to lose. I have never taken money I didn't feel belonged to me or not paid for services that were actually rendered, but I have yet to lose a dispute that I have taken on. This chapter comes from countless encounters with big companies, utility companies, credit card companies, and others.

Let's go over the basics first. These are the basics to keep in mind when you try to get some of YOUR money back from these companies.

Filing System—First, you need to have a good filing system. Lost billing statements, or even more importantly, lost sales receipts are the perfect excuse for a company not to accept your return or honor your dispute. You must keep paper copies of the things that matter in these situations. For billing companies, a copy of the statement should suffice.

Preparation/Organization—Whenever you make a phone call regarding a dispute, you need to have a pen and paper in your hand at all times. Keep in mind that a lot of times you will have to call back more than once to get your situation resolved. Therefore, every time you make a phone call in a particular situation, you need to write down the date and time of the conversation, a brief re-cap of what was said, and most importantly the name and position of the person you spoke to. Early on, I found that this was the easiest way for companies to avoid honoring my disputes. Or it would at least make it much more difficult to take care of. I would usually get something like:

"Well, sir. If you don't know who you talked to about this situation then there's not really much else that I can help you with." Of course, in reality, this means nothing and is nothing more than an excuse to not help you. Once I learned this, I even some times played a game with these people. I would "pretend" to not know who I spoke with the first time, just waiting for their stupid little excuse. As soon as they came out with it (and they always did) I would usually hit them with something like, "OK, actually I do remember who I spoke to. It was Jane in your Accounting Dept. and we spoke on February sixth... SHE told me blah blah blah and asked me to follow up with you about it." The silence on the other end of the line was usually deafening.

Also, you need to be prepared. You need to know exactly what the error was (being double-billed, un- authorized charge, etc.)

and you need to know what you're talking about. These people also seem to prey on ignorance. If they get the least sense that you don't know what you're talking about, they will pounce on it and be even less likely to help you. You also need to know what you want. Obviously, if you were double-billed or something, you would just want the charge taken off. But, in the cases I outline here in a minute, sometimes there is not an exact amount that needs to be fixed. Maybe you were just incredibly inconvenienced by somebody's crappy customer service, or something subjective like that. In these situations, here is what you need to do. You need to know what you want. For example, you paid $500 for some bedroom furniture that was delivered late, and so you're expecting a $100 credit from them. Now, here is the most important part. I am sure you have heard somewhere the phrase regarding any negotiation about money. It goes something like, "Whoever speaks first, loses." Keep this in mind.

When you call, have in mind what you want, but don't tell them unless you have to. Sometimes, you will end up with more than you originally wanted. Because at some point in time, somebody from the other end is going to ask you what you want.

For example, if you inquire about something that you think you deserve compensation for, and it finally gets to the point of how much you're going to be compensated, if *they* ask *you*, a bad response would be that you want a $100 credit. (Why? Because maybe they had in mind giving you a $200 credit).

A good response would be, "I don't know, how have you compensated customers in the past who have gone through the same thing I did?"

Then, if they offer something less than your expectation, counter with yours, and tell them why. Maybe they offer you a $50 gift certificate on a future purchase. I would say "Well, I have no immediate plans of buying any more furniture in the near future, and also, I think the compensation needs to be closer to $100 for the following reasons."

Willingness to Act—Pardon my French, but you need to have the balls to do something about these situations. Do not just "let them go." This goes back to the "It's your money, treat it that way" thing I was talking about earlier. When I first figured out how to win these kinds of disputes and always get what I want, I never really thought about telling anyone else about it. I told my parents and my family to an extent, and most of the time I just got looks from them like I was doing something that they themselves could never ever do. And now lately, since I began to share these techniques, I have even gotten responses from people like, "Oh, I could NEVER do that myself." Or, "Wow, you're so good; I wish I could do that." Well, I am no big brave guy or overbearing or anything like that. I am just treating my money like it's mine and I'm fighting like hell to get it back when someone is trying to take it from me unfairly.

To sum it all up, some final thoughts on the "balls" category. You need to also introduce what I like to call "veiled" threats during these discussions or letters. Of course, they are not real threats of harm or violence, no, to the contrary. Let me explain. And let me also say that they are a vital part of the process or the people you are speaking to will not take you seriously.

The first thing you want to say is that you are a very good customer and you have always been satisfied with the company's services/products in the past. And of course, you are quite upset that this current situation has happened to you. Now, obviously, you only go the route of the veiled threat if you see you're not getting anywhere by just reasoning with them. If you need to, you can also say that you would hate to have to look somewhere else to buy your furniture or your plane tickets or whatever the case may be. Not all companies have figured it out yet, but most have—they HATE to lose customers!!

Still not getting anywhere? You need to keep on track. You need to then go into some sort of explanation like this—and you can tailor it to your own needs. I usually say something like, "Look, I am just trying to be honest with you. I have been a good customer for your company over the years (of course, only say this if it is true. If not, simply say that you plan to be a good customer of theirs over the next several years.) Also, I am a very loyal customer to the companies I do business with. When I find a good company I stay with them, and many times pay more than the competition because of this loyalty. In addition, I also like to share information with my friends, family, and email contacts about my experiences with companies. And I can assure you, that I detail these experiences, both good and bad, with as many people as I can. I do that because I want to help build the businesses of companies that do things right and I also want to warn my friends and family and email contacts about companies that do not care about their customers."

Not to get off the point, but again, none of this is not true, and none of it is lies. I believe these things and although I may embellish them a little, they are all true. Usually, when you say this piece, it drives a stake through them and they become much more willing to help. Especially, always add the piece about email contacts. A lot of companies don't realize it but, you could send out a form letter of a bad experience with them and have it reach your entire email address book with just a few clicks. And I always tell them how easy it is and how I will definitely be doing it if there is not some sort of satisfaction on my part.

And finally, if your situation is serious enough and involves enough money and you are that upset about it, you can always threaten legal action. Again, I only use this in the most serious of cases, and have probably only used it once or twice, but sometimes it is necessary to get people to wake up. Once these companies hear the word "attorney," and if they know they are wrong, you are again liable to get them to wake up and actually work to take care of you. And I always mention my "attorney" very nonchalantly. I wouldn't suggest saying to the person you are speaking with that "since I'm not getting anywhere with you I am just going to sue you." Better yet, I usually say something like "Well, in the conversations that I have had with my attorney about this, he assured me that he could move forward with this if I choose to do so."

One final note: You always want to remain calm and collected and with an even voice during these discussions. Never use foul language and try not to lose your temper because a lot of people will simply stop listening to you if you start ranting and raving. Also, when you say a lot of these things in a calm voice, people realize that you're not just saying them, but that you mean them and you really will do them. I cannot say I have never lost my temper during these issues, I can only tell you that it doesn't solve anything and a lot of times makes it more difficult for you to get what you want.

Another important point to keep in mind is that you have got to stand up for yourself—when it is worth doing. If I find a mistake where someone has overcharged me by one dollar, I may just let it go. However, if you have been overcharged or expected to pay for something that you don't think you should or any one of a hundred other examples, you simply have got to stand up for yourself.

Sometimes, you have got to be willing to raise your voice (when necessary) and you have got to know the right things to say. If you know when and where to do it, raising your voice will sometimes worek in your favor. Basically, you have got to be willing to fight for your money and you have got to know how to fight to win. I know this sounds a little contradictory, but believe it or not, sometimes, raising your voice is beneficial. It is a little hard to explain, and you really have to feel out the person on the other end. To be honest with you, this is exactly how I found out that this works. A few times, I have become so upset in these situations that I have found myself speaking in a raised voice not because of some part of my grand plan, but merely because I was so upset about how I was being treated. And, usually, a few minutes into my speaking in this raised tone, I am thinking to myself—"You know what, if I were this person I would have already told me to lower my tone or we won't continue the conversation." In some instances, I never heard this and I got results. Of course, I don't suggest going into a possible dispute with this one at the top of your list of strategies, because most times it doesn't work.

So here we go with my examples. I think they are all very much worth reading, because each example pretty much corresponds to one of the basics that I outlined earlier. I think you will find them all interesting and relevant. The first one is an experience with a furniture company that goes hand in hand with preparation/organization.

Many years back, I had purchased some bedroom furniture from a certain company that allows you to pay off your purchase over an extended period of time. I will not name the company just to be on the safe side. So, you go and pick out your furniture, and unless you have a way of getting it home yourself, you have to schedule a delivery date. So, I did and I got my delivery date for a few days in the future.

I had just moved into my new house and was excited about getting my new bedroom furniture. I had actually already moved my old bed into an extra bedroom, had all the sheets ready and everything.

Well, since this was several years ago, and I can't remember if they did the thing where they say they will show up in some four-hour time block, or if it was an exact time or what it was. Anyways, by about five o' clock that day, they still had not showed up. I also can't remember if I took the day off for this or what, but at the least, I imagine I had to rearrange my work schedule for that week.

Around five-thirty, I called them, and I was fairly upset. I mean, who wouldn't be? Whoever I got on the phone apologized profusely, telling me it was just a mistake, and said they would be out the next day. If memory serves me correctly, they came the next day and dropped off my new bed.

This could be the end of the story, right? In my opinion, it shouldn't have been, and it wasn't.

Before I continue, let me also say that some of the tactics that I employ or methods that I use and am about to tell you about, may seem unethical or unfair. Let me tell you how I feel. I only want what I think I rightfully deserve from any company that I take on. I never blatantly lie to a company nor do I do anything illegal to get them to take some action. The reason why I do the things that I do is that most of these companies are huge, and to be honest with you could really care less about individual consumers. Well, they do care, but they certainly are not going to go the extra mile for anything or anybody. How many times do costs and other things that are incurred by companies simply get passed on to consumers. Who do you think pays for items that are shoplifted, to name an example? Ultimately, it is us, the consumer.

So, this is my basic mindset when dealing with these companies.

To proceed with the story, this was one of the first times I actually took on a company in a situation like this. Let's see, they did apologize and they did bring out the furniture the next afternoon, so I could have just been satisfied with that. Well, guess what? I wasn't.

And let me tell you why. I paid for the furniture and I also paid for the delivery and I paid for it to be delivered at the time they said it would be delivered. They did not live up to their obligation. I was also inconvenienced because I had already prepared everything to be able to sleep in my new bed that night. My old spring mattress and frame and everything else were thrown in an extra bedroom, so one could say that I basically had no bed to sleep in that night. Finally, I may not have actually had to take off work and lose wages for them to deliver it but I did have to rearrange my schedule. All in all, they did not live up to their delivery obligation and they inconvenienced me as a consumer on about three different levels. I felt I deserved some compensation for this inconvenience.

At first they did not feel the same way. I called back and spoke to the customer service department, and if I remember correctly was told that since they did eventually deliver the furniture, that they did not see any other recourse for me. They were not mean about it or anything and neither they nor I raised our voices, but they were unwilling to do anything about it. When I get turned away at this point, I do not lose hope or give up; it just makes me more determined.

Next, I looked up their home office address and I think I also was able to find the name of the vice president of customer service. I wrote a letter addressed specifically to him. This is also another good piece of advice. If you ever decide to write a letter, find out a specific person's name (preferably a higher-up in customer service) and address it specifically to them.

I won't go through the entire letter, because most of it explained what I just said to you about how they did not live up to their delivery agreement and I was also inconvenienced in numerous ways.

It was then that I pulled out my first technique. After I explained my story, I included a section in my letter that went something like this:

"Now, for right now, this matter is between you and me, and I hope that we can come to a mutually agreeable solution.

I can tell you that I am a fiercely loyal customer and when I feel that I am taken care of, and I will remain loyal forever. However, when I feel that I am wronged by a company I feel like it's my duty to tell others of my experience. And, with the advent of the internet and emails and everything else, my ability to communicate this story to a large number of people could be done by simply pressing a few buttons. I think I have about a hundred contacts in my email address book, and think of all the contacts in those people's address book.

"I think I deserve some compensation in this matter. I am only asking for what I think I rightfully deserve. You can choose to try to work this out, or I can communicate my somewhat disappointing experience with your company to as many people I can. The choice I yours. I will refrain from taking any action, for thirty days. Hopefully, I will have heard from you by then."

And then I included my contact information.

I mailed the letter and I waited. After about one week I got a phone call. It was from a senior CS rep from that company. They never mentioned the letter, but I know they got it. They said they were merely following up on what happened to me. I recounted the story again, I told them I still wasn't satisfied, and I told them I thought I deserved some compensation. Well this person then just straight out asked me how much was I talking about. This part threw me a little (which goes back to my section on preparation) and I think I eventually said I thought I deserved $100. (And this is probably about right for what I went thru. After all, I paid more than $1,000 for all of the furniture). She put me on hold for a few minutes, got back on and said it was approved and I got my money in about another week. I never forwarded my complaint to all of my friends and I have bought a great deal more furniture from that company since then.

Moving on to one of my more recent experiences with an airlines. This goes along with exhausting all possibilities and NEVER, NEVER giving up, and a filing system as well.

My wife recently scheduled an international trip for herself and my son to Moscow, Russia. We did it through the airlines that we fly often and that I have been fairly loyal to over the years. They have fallen on quite hard times recently, though. I had always heard that children fly for free up to the age of two, and thought that this would apply to my son. This was my first mistake– not having the facts. Parts of this story do not have much to do with my core dispute, I am just mentioning it to outline to you other steps you can take to prevent it from happening to you; this piece would be always having your facts. On the day we were to fly, I called and found out that I had to purchase a ticket for him. How much would that cost, I asked? Well, guess what? They couldn't tell me. The best answer I got was ten percent of a full fare plus "all applicable taxes and fees". The person on the phone was unable to give me an estimate on the mysterious "applicable taxes and fees".

(No surprise here, folks—when the CC bill came, the charges for my son's ticket were close to $400, and my wife's full fare only cost a little over $900. Again, get all your facts and you won't have that problem).

We got to the airport on the day they were supposed to leave, and as part of the check-in process, they were given one of those little ticket books that they used to issue about 500 years ago before e-tickets and paperless tickets. They never really mentioned too much about it, just issued a little book-let for my wife and my son. Off they went. The trip was two weeks long, my wife was not flying with anyone else, so as you can imagine, it was a hectic time for her to be doing all of this alone. She was lucky enough to be able to keep track of our son, much less all of her items and luggage.

They both enjoyed their two weeks over there tremen-dously and soon it was time to return. She went to the airport and realized that she had lost the little boarding pass booklet for my son's return flight. Keep in mind that this is a piece of paper that is probably four inches by two inches. Then, to her shock and amazement, she finds out from the representa-tives there that my son will not be able to board the plane without this little piece of paper. They claimed that they had "no proof" of the first leg of his flight. Basically, I guess what they were claiming was that our two-year-old son had simply been roaming the streets of Moscow for an indeterminate peri-od of time, and my wife finally decided to go over there and get him!

My wife, not knowing what to do, called me. Under other circumstances, this may have been one where we could have just fought it out right there at the airport, but it was an international flight, and in addition to that, the visas of both my wife and my son expired that day. In other words, she and our son had to get on the plane. She called to ask me what to do, and with the time change it was about 4:00 a.m. for me. I just told her to buy another ticket for our son in order to get home and we would straighten it out when they returned.

That's what they did. The one-way return flight for my son cost $562.

Shortly after they returned, I contacted the customer service department of the airlines. I told them that I had proof on my credit card statement that a round-trip ticket was purchased for my son. They were polite, asked me to fax that statement and I think some other information over to them. They told me they would need a few weeks to resolve it, but they gave every indication that it would be taken care of without incident.

It all went downhill from there. Two weeks went by and no one called me back. This, I think, is one tactic on these companies' part to get you to give up. Well, you just can't. You have got to be persistent. I called customer service and they told me that the whole issue had been sent over to their refunds department. I hung up and called the refunds department (keep in mind the approximate ten- to fifteen-minute wait each time these phone calls are made). And this is what the refunds department told me.

Basically, they could care less that I had proof of a ticket being purchased for my son. Based solely on the fact that my wife had lost that one little boarding pass, that one little piece of paper that measured about two by four inches, that there was nothing they could do. Now, this is when I lost my temper, which is honestly one thing you really don't ever want to do. Some reps will listen to you, but your chance of getting a favorable resolution goes down dramatically when you lose your temper. However, there is a difference between losing your temper and raising your voice. It is a fine line but there is a distinction. I should have just raised my voice, but instead lost my temper. I told them that wasn't good enough, I wanted my refund processed immediately, I don't care about their policies, and this is ridiculous etc.

After being told to calm down by the person on the other end (something else you never want to happen because it means now that subconsciously they have become dead set against doing anything to help you), I asked to speak to her supervisor. So, I was getting back on track. Her supervisor came on. I had already calmed down and I explained my story to her in its simplest terms. Then, I asked her 1) if it made sense to her that I was upset, and 2) is there anything at all that could be done? I told her I understood her policies and procedures, but also asked her to understand the unfairness of being charged $562 for losing a little piece of paper.

She put me on hold for a few minutes, came back on told me she had good news. Good news for her, I guess. She told me that she had gotten permission from her supervisor to treat this as a "lost ticket." (Wow, what a shocker. What else would it be treated as?) All I would have to do is to complete a Lost Ticket Application and I would be refunded my money and she would be happy to mail this form off to me. It all sounded great to me. That is, until the application came in the mail. At the top or somewhere on the form, they had written in that there would be a $100 processing fee. I think I was in shock for several minutes before it sank in.

$100?

One hundred dollars?

They were trying to tell me that it would take someone sooooo long, and that it would be sooooo difficult to process an application that had no more information on it besides my son's name, the original ticket number we bought for him and the new ticket number, that they would have to charge me an extra $100 for it?

And, on top of everything else, this was not even mentioned to me when I was speaking with the lady on the phone about it.

This really got my juices flowing. Looking back on it, it was probably a newer tactic created by these companies desperate to screw their consumers. They start out with trying to screw you out of a ton of your money. And if that doesn't work they break it down to a much smaller (but still unfair) amount. I guess that way they think that you will think you're getting a deal and will be willing to donate your hard-earned money to them.

Well, not me.

At this point in time, the only thing that I was worried about was if there was an expiration date on my ability to make a claim on this one, because I knew this was going to take some extra effort, and I also knew that there was a good chance that there was something in some fine print somewhere about a deadline. I later found out that I had up to one year from the purchase date of the ticket, so I knew I was OK.

This was a huge airline, and trust me, the bigger the company, the more difficult it is to beat them. Let me re-phrase that: the more difficult it is to claim back what is rightfully yours. This was a tough one, and an expensive one. At the moment, I was out $562. Of course, I could get back $462 of it, but I was going for what was rightfully mine, the full $562.

After I found out the name of the VP of Customer Service, I wrote him a long letter. I detailed the entire story to him, and simply asked if there was something that could be done about it. Basically, it was the same thing that I did in the furniture company situation.

This company, at the moment, was in deep financial trouble, and actually, on the verge of bankruptcy. I am sure this had something to do with how my situation played out. I had also researched the Internet to see if there were a lot of other complaints about them in general with respect to billing and customer service, and as it turns out, they were rampant. This airline was definitely in a tailspin, pardon the pun.

I enthusiastically sent my letter off, hoping for the same result as my first example. Do you know what kind of response I received?

Nothing. Absolutely nothing.

I didn't even get a form letter from a secretary or anything! It was then I knew I was really in for a battle if I wanted my final $100 back, but I still felt pretty good that I did have an option to at least get most of my money back if everything else failed.

I employed a technique that I never used before, but is at your disposal and is actually quite effective.

I disputed the purchase of the return ticket with my credit card company.

Now let me explain a few things so we are absolutely clear on them. First, your credit card company would be happy to dispute any kind of purchase that you would like them to. They know what to do, they can offer you advice, and they have dealt with hundreds of types of situations before, and either I was real lucky in the people I was able to speak with, or they really know what they are doing.

The only bad part is that disputing a charge takes some time to play out. Sometimes it can be several months before it is resolved. And, if you dispute a purchase before it is paid for and lose, you WILL have to pay the extra finance charges on it. So, be careful what you dispute, because there is some risk involved. I would always ask your credit card company for clarity on this as different policies may exist for different companies.

But, at this point in time, I was so mad at this airline that I was willing to take the risk because any finance charges that I may have had to pay would have been worth it just to cause them hassle and extra work. That may sound spiteful, but they caused me a huge amount of hassle and work and time when if they had just treated me fairly and correctly from the beginning we would not have been in such a mess.

After speaking with the rep from the credit card company, she advised me to do three things. First, wait before I send off the lost ticket application. If I did that, the whole thing would be over. Second, dispute half the amount of the original ticket that I bought for my son, because the airline never provided the goods and services they promised to on the second half of the flight. Third, dispute the entire price of the second ticket. I can't remember the technical reason she gave for disputing, but basically, it was because I should not have had to buy the ticket in the first place.

I submitted all of the documentation necessary to the credit card company, and the battle had begun. The documentation needed was basically proof that I had purchased both tickets, and a written version of my side of the story. Then, the credit card company takes it from there. But again, as I said, the process does take some time. It was probably about thirty days later that I finally heard back. And, not surprisingly, my claim was denied for the dispute on the second ticket I bought. The explanation given to the credit card company from the airline was that as soon as my son set foot on that plane returning from Moscow, that constituted the delivery of promised services (or some other technical phrase) and therefore, they had won *that* dispute.

But that was OK, because again, I was still determined. I called back the credit card company, and I actually had developed a pretty good relationship with the rep handling my case by now, and we talked about what to do. By the way, these reps are far from information processors or people without opinions just doing their jobs. They often can offer up good advice and strategies on how to win. Of course, they themselves only do this when they see the consumer has been wronged, but they can be allies to your cause as well.

So we were left now with only being able to attempt to get my money back for the return ticket bought for my son. Since they claimed that my son did in fact use his return flight from Moscow, and that they had no liability for that fare, then obviously, they never delivered the services on the second half of the round trip ticket we purchased for him originally. There was basically nothing they could say about that.

Since the original fare was right around $400, we disputed $200 of it and I submitted more documentation. We also decided to go ahead and submit the lost ticket application as well because if we lost this latest dispute, that would be the best-case scenario for me. So I went ahead with both things.

As luck would have it, I won my claim on the second half of the original fare, and received a check for $200 from the credit card company. And, believe it or not, the airlines ultimately ended up honoring the lost ticket application as well, so I got another $462 back from them.

Now, if you do the math, I technically ended up getting an extra $100 out of the whole thing. I also know that I have stated before that I only want what is rightfully mine. Well, guess what? I felt that this extra $100 was rightfully mine. My wife and young son were put through a load of unnecessary stress and worry that day at the airport, and with my fight with the airline and time invested in pursuing two disputes and the lost ticket application, I had no problem in getting this extra $100.

One other thing, to finish the story. During the course of looking through all of the charges from the airline for this trip, I was also able to uncover approximately $150 of other unnecessary charges put on my credit card by the airlines for things ranging from extra baggage fees that did not belong there to currency transaction fees that they tried to assess because it was an international flight.

Moral of the story: Keep an eye on your credit statement, and fight like hell when someone tries to take your money.

My final little story, but another big one, illustrates the virtues of persistence (and also the need for a filing system). It was against some sort of an X-ray or analytical medical company. I think they analyzed blood or X-rays or something. It was almost three years ago, so I have forgotten some of the details.

Anyways, this relates back to the pregnancy of my wife. I could probably write another book on how to keep track of all the bills that come your way during a pregnancy, but I'll limit myself to this one little example. Suffice it to say, that you really need to look at ALL of the bills coming in during this time, because you're either paying for them out of pocket or through your insurance, so you are still fighting for your money if you find an error. The best advice I can give you is when in doubt, call and ask questions. I was able to find several errors on my own during our pregnancy. This particular error I found was to the tune of over $400.

During the pregnancy, a slew of bills came to our house. I did check almost all of them (at least the ones I could understand with all of their technical billing jargon), but the ones that really caught my eye had the statement that said "insurance has paid everything they're going to pay; now you owe us the rest." Then, I really took a look at it.

The bill in question did not really come to my house until around August of 2006, but the date on it was way back in March of 2006. The bill was for well over $400 and again, it was from some diagnostic company.

To be honest with you, I waited for a few months before I even called them about it. I figured it was something that insurance hadn't paid for yet, it was sent to my home mistakenly or a variety of other things. These things do happen from time to time, and I was tired of calling about every single bill only to be told that insurance would still be paying it or it was a mistake, or it wasn't really a bill, or whatever. I assumed that this one was just going to iron itself out.

Around August, I began receiving steady monthly notices from this company claiming that I owed them the $400-plus. So I contacted them around September or October.

Without giving too detailed an explanation, this is what I found out when I called. The bill WAS my responsibility, because insurance didn't cover it. The information on the bill was in medical terms that I could not understand, so the explanation that I got from the X-ray/diagnostic place was that these items were not covered by insurance because they were of a "preventive" nature and not of a "diagnostic" nature. Again, mostly not too understandable for me, but at this point it sounded like I really owed the money.

And then...

...I got to thinking about it.

My wife gave birth in December of 2006. If this bill was from March of that year, then it had to be right around the time when we first went to the doctor. So, after discussing it with my wife and looking at the calendar, we finally realized that these charges related all the way back to our very first visit to the doctor.

So then...

...I got to thinking again.

I thought, well, if this was from our very first doctor's visit, the one where we actually confirmed that she was pregnant, then what possibly could have been done that was of a "preventive" nature? Wouldn't it all have been "diagnostic"? Again, I am no medical expert, I was just using common sense, but I thought I had a case. I called them and told them what I thought, and they said they would look into it. They said they would call me back in a week. They never did. I called them back after two weeks, and they said that no, I still owed the money. I told them I wasn't going to pay, so they told me they would start another "investigation." Honestly, I doubt they ever investigated anything because I went through that sham three times and it all came back with the same result—I still owed them the money. The reason that they gave was that they do not issue the "codes" for charges to their company, that the doctor's office where we visited issues the codes. Well the codes on that bill were for "preventive" care, soooooo, I still owed them the money.

Well, once again, not good enough for me.

I called the doctor's office where we went. They told me that of course it was all "diagnostic" stuff done that day, but also, according to the date of the bill that I was calling about, it was billed one day before our actual appointment, and we had billable stuff sent to the diagnostic place that had already been paid by insurance, so this must have been a clerical issue. OK, great, so back to the diagnostic company.

They said they had to do another investigation, which this time, I think they actually did. It took them about a month but they came back and told me that the date listed on my bill was probably just a clerical error. The charges that were paid for by insurance were valid, and the charges they were trying to get me to pay for were valid as well. We were now back to square one again.

Before I continue, let me tell you that once again, I think the way a lot of this stuff plays out with these companies is either one of the ploys I mentioned with the airline incident, or this one—I think they just try to wear you down till you give up and pay. Don't ever give in! Don't ever give up! Remember, it's your money, treat it that way.

I'll speak in a minute about exactly which battles to under-take, but let's continue this story. Now, I was mad. I had invested far too much time into this thing, and I was convinced that I did not owe this money. Like I told you with the airline story, it is good to be able to get in touch with someone who empathizes with your story and who might actually go an extra mile to assist you. In that case, it was the lady from the dispute department at the credit card company. Here, it was a lady I finally reached at the doctor's billing office. If I remember, I actually had to send her a registered letter until she would actually return my phone calls because at first, she just wouldn't even call me back. Yes, I sent her a registered letter. At this point, I was getting a little desperate and in danger of losing my perfect record! (I have never, ever lost one of these things that I have taken on.) This woman at the doctor's billing office who I had a pretty good idea could help me a little more, at first would not return my phone calls. The registered letter worked. I told her my whole story (I embellished a little but I never lied). I told her that I was convinced that I did not owe this money. I told her if I had to pay the money then it would become quite difficult to put food on the table for my baby (not a lie!). I told her all the other bills that I knew I was responsible for were already crushing me, and this one would kill me (again, not a lie!).

The letter worked. The next time I called her, she called right back. I told her straight out that I thought this stuff was coded wrong. She dug in and investigated the codes herself. Yes, they were "preventive" codes. So, actually, the diagnostic company was not even trying to rip me off, they were just charging me what they thought I owed them. My new confidante then dug in and researched exactly what was done at our doctor's visit, just to be sure. Yes, it was all of a "diagnostic" nature. Then, she went the extra mile (remember, this lady works in "billing") and found out that the results of our visit had actually been sent to my wife's gynecologist's office for review—*and that is ultimately where they were mis-coded.*

I called my wife's gynecologist's office, got in touch with their billing office, told them the entire story, and finally, convinced someone there to re-code this bill (by now is was the following April, so this whole thing had gone on for more than a year). The bill was re-coded (which took all of about two minutes to be done) and after all was said and done; I got a final bill from the diagnostic company for a grand total of $2.36.

Two dollars and thirty six cents.

Down from something that was over $400. Using my time work comparison, that one was worth almost a week's worth of work!

No one can tell me that one was not worth fighting for.

And it all came down to persistence.

Now the thing that I will conclude with is when to take on these types of what I call "challenges." I don't know what you're cut-off point is, but mine is usually around $10. Of course, if it happens from someone or some company that has made me mad, I may make a big deal out of $5 just to cause them some of my pain as well, it just depends. Would that be considered spite? If so, so be it. I consider it getting tired of having to defend my money all the time. Ten dollars may sound a little low to you, but I would say that most of the time, ten dollars is worth fighting for. I hate to repeat myself, but—it's your money, treat it that way.

I have found two- and three-dollar mistakes on my credit cards before. A tip mis-entered at a restaurant or something like that. Usually, I let that go. If it is a five-dollar mistake and it is going to take me an hour to rectify it, well, I have better things to do with that hour.

One other thing about disputing. Whenever possible, always try to dispute the charge before you pay the bill. Many times, you will hear that if you already paid the bill, then it is not eligible to be disputed. I found out in the case of the airline that this is not entirely true. I am not sure in which cases you can dispute a charge that's already been paid, but in my specific example, I was able to. But it is a good idea to recognize these errors before the bill is paid and to dispute them before you pay out any money. Of course, if you are checking your statements each month like you should be, you would recognize any and all errors before paying your bills anyways!

This concludes my section on ways to spend less money in your life. Again, there are some specific concrete things you can do in your life, but for the most part it involves a shift in your mindset. You really have to "take control" of your money, realize that you do work hard for it, and fight just as hard when someone tries to take it from you unfairly.

Those are the basics, the "must-dos" before you call any utility company, credit card company, or anybody else that you might call for a possible dispute over your money. Yes, I'll say it again, *your* money. You have to understand that this game is all about information. And whoever has the most of it usually wins. So you want to have as much information as you possibly can. Remember, these companies, for the most part, do not want to pay you your money, or if you call them to mention a possible error, they will first do the best that they can to convince you that you are mistaken, and then, usually, they will do the best they can to make it as difficult as possible for you to get your money back.

Now, in all honesty, some of the statements that I just made are exaggerations. But they are the thoughts that I have in my mind every single time I call these people just to keep my guard up. Most times, when an error is recognized, it is usually fixed in a decent period of time. However, you need to be prepared for ALL of those other times. This is the best way that I have found to do it.

Now, we will move on to ways that you can actually generate some extra cash in your life.

CHAPTER 5

Generating Income

"Formal education will make you a living; self-education will make you a fortune." -Jim Rohn

Now that we've gone through all of the "saving" stuff, let's get on with some "money making" stuff. What I mean is that training yourself to turn down your thermostat and cutting out coupons and all of that other stuff is essential, but it is also not very glamorous. And also, it's not like you are getting a check from any of these people, so you're really just lowering your expenses or letting less money out of your wallet. I'd like to move on now to some ways that you can actually generate money in your current life.

I want to be clear about the fact that it has nothing to do with changing jobs, or working a second job, or even spending every bit of your free time trying to generate some extra pennies. I have applied my time/work theory to this situation as well.

Basically, if I cannot generate at least as much income as I make at my regular job, then to me, it is not worth doing. I would rather spend the time with my son or my wife. Depending on how much of a commodity "free time" is in your life, it may dictate how you decide to rate this. If you are single and possibly somewhat "bored" in your spare time, maybe you will put the cutoff point at $10 per hour. Then again, maybe if spare time is at quite a premium in your life, maybe you will set the bar higher. It is entirely up to you. The point is that there are a lot of things that you can do in your life right now to help you actually put more money in your wallet/purse. And with a lot of them, you can start today.

Let me begin with things that you can do without spending one bit of your spare time. Then we will go from the lesser income generating ideas all the way up to the top.

Now, you ask, how can I make more money in my life without using any of my spare time? It is simple.

I have worked in management for the better part of my professional life, and I have enjoyed it quite a bit. The part I enjoy about it the most is not the fact that I get to order people around or tell them what to do. Honestly, it's to the contrary. Actually, that's the part of the job that I hate the most. What I enjoy the most is being able to teach people things. I think I possess the god-given talent of being able to show people how to do things, and how to do them well. That's what I like the most about management. However, there was one thing that always puzzled me which was when my employees told me they weren't making enough money, or they needed to make more or they haven't had a raise in so much time, etc.

This is the question or the problem that is most common with almost all workers today—they don't make enough money. What puzzled me about it was this: the employees that typically complained about this the most usually had one or more of the following characteristics:

1) Had a problem with being on time for work.
2) Were usually not my highest performers.
3) Usually had a tendency of complaining about most other things in addition to money.

And the list goes on....

Are you starting to get my point?

Because, whenever any employee of mine would ask me about when would he/she get another raise or how come he doesn't make more money, or he needs to make more money, etc, the first thing I would do is to check his time cards for the last few months. And typically, there would be quite a few instances where he/she did not show up on time.

Let's get out the calculator again and utilize the "times twelve" rule. Let's say you work forty hours per week making $10 an hour, and you have a problem showing up to work on time. For this example, let's say you average being fifteen minutes late to work, three times a week. That's forty-five minutes in lost wages per week—$7.50 per week. That translates into $30 per month, and $360 per year. So, there you go. Start showing up to work on time and you can put more than $350 in your wallet over the course of a year.

Now, the next typical characteristic of people who seem to always be asking me for more money is that usually, they were not my highest performers. That should be easy to understand, at least from a management perspective. That would be because my worst performers would eventually quit or get fired, and my best performers never really had to worry about money, because they were my best performers and I always did my best to take care of them financially and keep them happy. It was the "middle of the road-ers" that always seemed to be asking for more money.

So, the best way to make more money at your job is to be the best performer that you know how to be. In the restaurant business this did not always necessarily mean that you had to be the greatest cook or greatest dishwasher. There are a lot of ways to improve your performance at work, even if for some reason you are simply not able to be the very best at your actual position. One way is what we just talked about. ALWAYS be on time! Trust me, managers appreciate that and it does help you. Second, you can always do your best. Managers recognize this also. They probably realize that you might not be the very best cook in the building, but if they see that you are trying and putting forth your best effort every single day, they will recognize that also. Third, volunteer to learn new things or volunteer for extra projects. Sometimes, it may seem like there is nothing to do at your job. And this would probably apply to any job at any business. Well, if that's the case, ask your manager for more responsibility, ask them for extra projects, and ask to learn how to do something new. A good manager will always find something for you to do, and a good manager also greatly appreciates the type of employee who volunteers for extra things to do rather than them having to tell you to do these extra things.

Also, let your manager know that you are willing to work over-time whenever necessary. In most situations, there may not be a lot of it available, but if there is, and you can be available for it (meaning, you can work your schedule around it), tell them you'll do it. It is a fantastic way to increase your income!

And finally, one way to possibly generate more income without doing much different at your job is to, if applicable, stop complaining. What I mean is, if you are a complainer, stop it. I can tell you one thing that most good managers place quite a high importance on, and that is people who do not complain. You don't even have to be close to the best worker in the house, but if you do a good job, do it consistently, and are not com-plaining all the time, these things go a long way. What I am trying to tell you is that by discontinuing the complaining, you might be able to set yourself up for a raise or a bigger raise if you are already eligible for one.

Obviously, if something needs to be brought to your boss' attention, or something is really on your mind, by all means bring it to their attention. That's what they are there for. But there is a big difference between this and complaining. People that complain all the time rarely want to be a part of a solution to anything, because then it would eliminate the amount of things that they can complain about. It is not so much that they are desperately unhappy with their job; they just have an inher-ent need to complain, and to complain all the time. Managers hate this. And there are a lot more of this type of employee out there than you might realize.

If you do fall into this category and seriously decide to stop complaining—bring it to your boss' attention as well. If you do complain, they already know all about it. Just approach them and tell them you are making a conscious effort to stop complaining all the time. After they pick their chins up off the floor, they will probably watch you a little more, and if you follow through on your promise they will remember this at raise time. Those who do go down this road usually end up becoming much more productive employees after the complaining stops.

If you are unwilling to do any or all of the things above to help make yourself more money, there is also obviously the option of looking for another job. Of course, the opportunities and/or challenges in this area will depend on your area of expertise and your interests, but it can be done.

I want to talk about something else in this category before we go any further.

It is called happiness at your job, and it is very important. You have probably heard it said many times before that it is more important that you are happy at your job than it is how much money you make at your job. Well, this is obviously true for a lot of reasons. A great deal of our lives is spent at our jobs so of course it is important to have one that you like to do.

I can personally attest to this fact because toward the end of my career in restaurant management, I had really lost my passion for the business, I didn't really like what I was doing anymore, and to be honest with you, I was just collecting a paycheck. I put on a good enough face at this last job until I could change careers, but I really wasn't happy. If you have never been in this situation before, consider yourself lucky. Your job turns into a grind, it affects other areas of your life, and it can affect the people that are around you as well if you are not careful.

A recent study showed that fewer than half of all Americans are actually happy at their jobs. That's a pretty shocking statistic.

I don't know that I would ever give you advice about staying at a job that you are unhappy doing, but I guess I would put it like this. If you can stay at your current job that you are unhappy at because you make more money there than somewhere else, or if you can take a job making more money doing something that you may not necessarily like doing (on a short-term basis), then I would seriously consider doing it.

Personally, I had worked in the restaurant business for approximately twenty years. For the majority of that time, I was single. Therefore, it didn't really matter to me that I had to work over sixty hours a week a lot of the time, I had to work a lot of nights, I had to physically bust my butt most of the time, and everything else that goes along with working in that industry. For the better part of that time, I was married to my job, and that was OK. I loved working in that industry, towards the end I was making very good money doing what I was doing, I was good at what I did, and so on.

About five years from the end, I really started thinking that I wanted to do something else for a living. I just knew that I had other talents, and I knew there were other things I could be successful at. However, I never really pursued anything because the only real experience I could put on a resume was restaurant management, and I just always thought that it would be impossible to change industries.

Then I got married, and my eyes really opened up. I learned that there was this wonderful thing out there called a "personal life" that I had never enjoyed before. I learned that there was room in one's life for things other than your job, and a lot of them were actually fun to do.

I could go on and on. I knew that if my marriage was going to work, that I would more than likely have to change careers. I started looking around…and around and around. I was looking for almost three years. I went on tons of interviews, sent out millions of resumes, sought out the advice of anyone who would listen to me, and let me tell you, it was not very easy to find something. In a sense, I was right; there were not a whole lot of employers outside of the restaurant industry who were interested in me.

Now let me tie this in to the financial side of things. By this time, it was around 2004 or so, and I had basically been completely out of debt for about two or three years. I was still really enjoying the newness of being out of debt, of not wasting money, and just getting into the whole saving wherever I could, spending less, and just a little bit of generating more income.

My point is this—I knew that no matter how "unhappy" I might have been in the restaurant business, I was still making good money, and I also knew that I was going to continue to do that job until I could find something making AT LEAST the same amount of money. And that was probably one of the bigger reasons why I stayed in the restaurant business for three years after I was really unhappy in the industry—because of the money. Or actually, because of the lack of opportunities to make the same money if not better in another industry.

Sure, I could have gone into sales (where it's all commission-based and not a steady salary) or restaurant equipment sales or the liquor industry or a variety of other jobs, but they did not pay as well. So, I stayed. And I stayed until I found something making just about right at what I was making when I left the restaurant industry.

The reason is this—and trust me on this, because I've been in both spots:

The unhappiness that I was enduring by working at a job that I did not necessarily love pales in comparison to the unhappiness and stress and everything else that goes along with being in debt, with not having money to do the things I wanted to do, and so on and so forth.

There is really no comparison. Working at this restaurant was not fulfilling. I lost my passion for the business like I said, and I was really just collecting a paycheck. I was still doing the best that I could but I had no drive for the business, and if you have ever worked in that industry, you know that without passion and drive it is virtually impossible to be successful.

But guess what? That paycheck that I was collecting was a pretty damn good one. And it allowed me to pay my bills on time with money left over. It allowed me to take my wife on vacations when we wanted to go, it allowed me to do all of the things I had been able to do the past few years since I was then out of debt.

A little unhappiness and non-fulfillment on the job is nothing compared to the monthly drain of having no money, being behind on bills, etc.

So, again, if you are less than thrilled with your current job, but can't find a better paying one, I would stay put until your financial house is in order. If you can switch jobs to bump up your income, even though it may be to a job you know you'd be less than thrilled doing, I would seriously consider doing it. The long-term happiness you can generate in your life by doing this on a short term basis, to me, is well worth it.

A lot of the things that I just wrote about are what gave me the motivation to start this project. Sure, I wanted to help people, and sure I thought that now might be the perfect timing for this type of project considering the state of our economy, but it also had a lot to do with my current employment situation. I am already doing the majority of the things that I wrote about in the first two thirds of this book and although I am learning new ways all the time to save money, I have the basics of it down to a science. As far as generating income in my spare time, there was not much else I could do. I was already doing all of the things that I am about to go over.

But I have always had a passion for writing and I have always had a passion for teaching people things that I have learned over the years. What a better combination to tie into writing a book, right?

Those are the main reasons why I took on this project—I love to write, I love to help people, and I love to teach people new things. I think I love this part so much because I absolutely love to learn new things. And, of course, I would be telling a big lie if I said that I did not hope to be able to generate some income through this project. So, there you have it. How about that for a self-fulfilling prophecy? I wrote this book because of the things that I talk about in this book. Pretty neat stuff if you ask me!

I guess just to tie this thing all together, one of the other reasons why I decided to take on this project is because I am not exactly the happiest person on Earth with my current full-time job and it is far from a "dream" job. I like working there (I am basically a bi-lingual manager at a Hispanic financial institution), and the hours are alright and the pay is pretty good, but it never was something that I wanted to do for the rest of my life. Remember, the main reason why I took that position was because it allowed me to improve my quality of life by no longer having to work sixty-plus hours a week, but it also allowed me to make the same amount of money.

But it is not like I derive any life-long happiness out of this position, so that is another reason why I took on this project. I will continue to work at that position until either this writing thing takes off into something that I can live off of, or until I can find something that makes me happier but still allows me to draw fairly close to the salary that I draw now.

Let's move on to more ways to try to generate some extra income in your life. For whatever reason, going out and finding a second job may not be an option. Maybe it is because of family concerns, maybe your primary job won't allow you to, or maybe you just don't want to work a second job, but you want to try to make some more money. I have a few solid suggestions for you. They are basic, simple, and fast, and can easily be fit in to the busiest of schedules. The more time you are able to invest in them, the more money you can make.

I will go over two of the easiest first. One is **filling out surveys** on the Internet. Of course, there are millions of sites out there that do this—but not many are worth your time if you are trying to generate extra cash. Most offer no incentives at all, some offer points to be added up over time that can be redeemed for prizes. And most of the sites that do this, offer so few points for each survey completed that it is really not worth your time. Now, time management in life is an entirely different issue, but the way I see it, you want to generate extra money in your life in the most time effective way possible.

How they work is that you sign up, fill out some brief biographical info and they begin sending you surveys based on your biographical make-up. When I first started doing this, I probably subscribed to five or six different sites. I later narrowed it down to only two over time—the two that are the most profitable for me.

One site gives you a varying amount of points based on the type of survey, and you can redeem your points for cash or other prizes as they add up. Most surveys are actually fairly interesting to do, some not so much, but it can eventually generate some decent cash for you over time. I made about $100 last year from this site alone. The actual site is www.lightspeedpanel.com

The second site is even better. They used to offer $5 per survey, but I think it is down to $3 per survey now, with a chance at a weekly drawing for $500. Still, this is pretty good. This idea is not meant to generate millions for you, but if you fill them out consistently it can create a decent amount of money for you over the course of a year. Also, from time to time they will actually send you products that are being tested (they're not even on the market yet) so this part can be quite fun. I have tested many things myself over the years, from disposable razors to canned soups and some other foods. This site is called www.pineconeresearch.com

Another way to REALLY start making some money in your spare time to consider starting your own business. If this sounds pretty daunting, it is not as big of a project as it might seem. The possibilities are endless, and if you approach it correctly and are committed and fairly talented in at least one area (aren't we all in at least one area?), then it can be quite profitable.

Of course, there is a right way and a wrong way to go about doing it. First, you need something that you can sell. This could be a product or a service. Believe me, everyone on Earth has something that can add value to another person's life. It is just a matter of how you harvest this talent and turn it into something sellable.

A friend of mine recently graduated college, had no desire of entering the real business world, and started a few ventures of her own with a great deal of success. That is the main reason why I included this section, because I know it can be done. She graduated with a degree in business, so what she ended up getting into was not completely related to her specialty. What

I am trying to say is that she found her passion, she acted on it, and in less than one year this was what she was able to come up with: www.dreamfollowers.com

Do not focus so much on the content of this site, rather the simple fact that this person was able to do this on her own, beginning with simple desire and determination. She later got into other ventures as well, and this has turned into a full-time career for her.

Let's move onto some other less time-consuming ways to generate cash in your life. I want to tell you a story about something that happened to me quite recently. It was not really supposed to be a part of this book, but it ended up being for obvious reasons. I guess it just goes to show you that as long as you keep a good head on your shoulders, and keep your eyes wide open, there are always new ways to be found in any of the three main categories of this book. This one happens to fall under the generating income section.

My wife recently finished her second bachelor's degree at our local state university, and if you have recently attended college or know someone who has, you more than likely know about the insane cost of textbooks. I became well aware of this insanity over the past few years because I would look at the credit card statements as they came in and my jaw would just drop to the ground when I saw the amounts charged to the bookstore.

I attended college many years ago and I remember books being expensive back then but not like this. To me, paying $40 for a textbook was unbelievable. That price would be considered a bargain at today's prices. I have heard of some books costing up to $200 apiece.

For the first few years, we did like most everybody else: We bought the textbooks, used them for the semester, and then at the end we sold them back to the bookstore where we bought them from (and probably got about fifteen percent of what we paid). The ones they would not take back simply piled up in one of our closets.

I was never too involved in this process until towards the end of her college career. It was one day when I saw how high the pile had gotten in our closet. I asked my wife about it and she said there was nothing she could do with them because the bookstore didn't want them back. She also had about four books from her last semester that needed to still be sold back.

I did a little thinking (that is, stopped being a mule), and this is what I came up with.

I thought that first, there must be some way that we could make more money from our old textbooks rather than just selling them back to the bookstore. And second, somebody somewhere must have some kind of use for the textbooks the bookstore said they no longer wanted. After a little research I found a large number of Web sites on the Internet that would buy back our textbooks, and I didn't even really have to do much research to realize that they paid much more than our local bookstore.

As I am sure you have already seen, I am not really into the business of promoting Web sites or anything like that, but

I would like to do a little of that here. The two that I found on the Internet that seem to do the best job and seem to pay the most money are:

www.bluerectangle.com

www.bookbyte.com

With both sites, you simply put your books in a box, attach the shipping label they provide for you and off they go. There is already a negotiated price given (you simply punch in the ISBNs and they tell you exactly what you're getting paid). You don't even have to take them to the post office; you just give them to your postman. The payment takes a while, but these two sites seem to do the best job in the way of convenience and in the way of how much they pay.

For a few semesters, at the end of each, I would punch in the numbers, decide between the two sites who would pay more, and send off the books. There were some books that even they didn't take, so I still had quite a pile in the closet. Again, I thought, there must be somebody somewhere who could use these books. That was when I came across Amazon.com

Of course, I had already been well aware of Amazon, but I simply knew them as an online retail store where you could buy things. I had purchased a few things from them before, and always knew them to be a pretty good site, one that had been around for a long time.

Somehow I discovered the idea of listing my textbooks on Amazon and selling them myself. At first, this sounded to me a lot like eBay, and I was never really too high on the idea of selling things on eBay. All of this is nothing more than personal opinion, because I know that there are thousands, if not millions of people out there who have made a great deal of money selling on eBay. It was just never something that appealed to me. Because it does take a lot of work, there is some risk involved, and it also takes a lot of time to do it right.

My main concerns for not wanting to go the eBay route is that you have to pay a listing fee for all of your items (meaning, you still have to pay eBay if you list something and it does not sell). Second, you have to keep track of bids and a few other things, and third as I have heard, eBay has been hit fairly hard by less-than-responsible sellers and buyers and a lot of rip-offs have occurred in the past. So, to make a long story short, eBay never interested me.

As I began to dig into Amazon, however, I learned quite a few things. First, you can open an account there with nothing more than your personal information, some simple name for your "store," and a bank account.

Second, and more importantly, there are no fees for listing items there. With eBay, you pay a listing fee whether the item sells or not; with Amazon, you only pay it when it sells. Also, there is no "bidding" with Amazon. You put the price you want to sell your item for, and you wait for it to sell. You can even look at what all the other similar items are selling for so you don't price yourself too high.

One small catch—you can only list things that have already been listed there (unless you pay to upgrade your account status).

But it is fairly difficult to find something that has not already been listed there, so for me, this was not much of an issue.

I quickly found out that I could in most cases make more money by putting my items on Amazon and waiting for them to sell rather than getting ripped off at the bookstore or even using one of the online used textbook sites. It took a few months, but all of my textbooks except for two sold, and I think I had almost twenty at the time. Even all the ones that neither the bookstore nor the online textbook sites wanted, I still found a buyer for. Granted, on some of them I didn't make more than a few dollars, but what was I going to do with them? With the newer textbooks, I made substantially more money selling them on Amazon than the other two options.

I was feeling pretty good about myself and the textbooks because I knew I made more money on them than I had in the past. Then, guess what? Yup, I got to thinking again.

I knew that I had several unwanted items around the house that were, for the most part, brand new or close to brand new. Most were gifts that I got that I never wanted or needed, and some were things that I bought and simply never used.

I think it started with a digital photo frame that I bought for my wife a few years previous that for whatever reason, she just never used. It still had the original box and all of the stuff that went with it, and it was just collecting dust. I threw caution to the wind and put it on Amazon. It was nothing special, and there was only one other like it listed on Amazon. I think the other one was priced at $40. Well, I probably could have played the "pricing game" a little bit more aggressively than I did, but my motivations were basically to make some money and to get rid of unwanted stuff. Therefore, I put a lower price on it than I normally would have. Plus, I really didn't know what I was doing at the time because it was all brand new to me. Well, that photo frame sold in less than two days.

They gave me two days to ship it (Amazon gives you a standard shipping credit, so sometimes you make a little extra money off of the shipping and sometimes you lose a little, but it's not much). I was shocked actually when I got the email that said to ship it.

Now of course, being the person that I am, I did not want to spend any money on shipping supplies. So, I simply took some of the paper bags that I get from one of my local grocers and turned them into packing supplies. I took the package with me to work, used the mailing tape there and I had my first official Amazon sale. I think I made $32 off of that digital photo frame—something that was just sitting around my house. And after I thought about it, I realized that I actually made money in another way too. I had purchased that frame for my wife at some Black Friday, day-after-Thanksgiving sale one year previous, and I actually paid only $25 for it. So, I doubly made money. Not too bad for a new guy, huh?

The floodgates opened from there. In the midst of selling my wife's textbooks, I probably listed and sold about thirty to forty other regular books that I had around my house. I also started opening closets, checking inside drawers, looking in the garage, etc. You would not believe the stuff that I found that I was able to sell there.

I sold an old 35mm camera that I found. I sold a globe, believe it or not, for about $30. I sold a cheap GPS system that I got for a Christmas gift that I never used. Let me see, what else? Some office organizer binders, some unused computer software, two pieces of car audio that I never used, a web cam, and the list goes on and on.

By the time it was all said and done, I had made almost $1,000 in approximately three months!! That's no exaggeration and no lie. It was unbelievable.

I continue to look for and find items in my house that I can sell, but not as many as before (most of the closets have been emptied!). Imagine what you might be able to find and how much money you could make, with very little work and time involved, by just opening some closets and drawers!

On the next Saturday that you find yourself with a little free time, start to "Amazon" your house. It's fun, and you'd probably be surprised at the money you can make!

Moving on, again, I am not really into the business of promoting Web sites, but here is another one that I have had quite a bit of success with. It's called:

www.Fatwallet.com

I should actually contact these guys, let them know I am promoting their site in my book, and see if I can make some money off of it. I mean, hey, it's free advertising for them, right?

Anyways, Fatwallet.com is a free Web site to join and they provide you with a wide variety of ways to save money.

It runs the gamut from anything from good coupons to get and print, or free rebate deals, to ways to actually make money from your credit cards. But that's only if you're credit card discipline is good enough. I'll get into all that in a later section. They also list all kinds of posts where you can get free useable stuff from the Internet.

It is hard to explain everything they offer on the site; the best way is to go and check it out.

I'll give you a recent example. I located a couple of fantastic deals on Fatwallet that involved laundry detergent. As I have said before, I have not really gotten deep into the couponing game, I really just pick and choose and only "kind of" pay attention to coupons. I came across two deals on Fatwallet, and they were both involving laundry detergent. At first, I thought I wouldn't even fool with it, but then I thought, well, I could care less what brand of laundry detergent I use, so if this deal will allow me to buy it cheaper than I already do, then why not?

I printed out the rebate form, bought the products, and at the end of the day, I wound up with $22 worth of free laundry detergent. Now, in the world of couponing and grocery shopping, a $22 savings is pretty substantial! It was enough laundry detergent for my household for about four months.

So if you have a moment, check out their website. It would be well worth your time and I would be quite surprised if you could not find at least one thing that would help you in at least one of the three main areas of this book.

MISCELLANEOUS—

Here are quite a few "little" things that I have incorporated into my life to generate extra income. Some of these may not apply to all, but I think it is all pretty good stuff.

Donate—Donating your unwanted items, or your money, to a qualified organization will not actually generate extra income for you, but it will allow you an additional tax deduction. I speak more about it in the chapter on taxes, I just wanted to mention it here because I am a firm believer in it.

Investing—I wanted to include just a short section on investing. First, this book is not about investing at all. Maybe that will be my next book, I don't know. The point is, once you have done most or all of the things that I have outlined in this book, you should find yourself with a decent amount of money in your bank account. What do you do with this extra money? The first thing I would tell you is that if you have made some major strides in your personal economy, and you are no longer wasting money, and you are stretching your dollars as much as they can be stretched, I would suggest giving yourself a pat on the back. Reward yourself! The whole point of this is not to save up a million dollars and never enjoy it or spend it. Make yourself happy! Had an eye on some particular item that you have been holding off on? Well, if you feel you can financially swing it, go ahead and buy it! You deserve it!

However, after this is done, it is time to make your money start working for you. That is probably another milestone in the "feel-good" events I have experienced through my own financial journey.

Before I got myself out of my financial mess I had created, I was working hard for my money. Very hard. After all of that, I decided it was time to get my money to work hard for me. If you can get to the point where you have extra money that you don't need to pay bills, you can get this money itself to generate more money for you. You just have to be smart about it. This is the basics of investing.

The first and best way to do this is through an employer-provided 401K plan.

The only thing you need to realize about this is that this needs to be money that you know you will not need until retirement. The reason I say this is that if it is money that you might need some day, there are substantial penalties for getting access to it. Also, there are other places you can put it if you think you might need it someday. However, you can set it up to where it is money that you never really notice. And it is a tremendous way to save for your retirement. It is a pretty simple process. A certain amount of money is taken out of your paycheck before the government takes taxes out, and it is invested for you. Usually, you have some control over which investments to choose, and really that is about it. Choose an amount you can definitely afford in the beginning, as you can usually adjust the percentage or amount taken out of your check at certain times of the year, or depending on your plan, whenever you want to. After that, simply watch your money grow!

There are other ways to get your money to work for you while still having access to it. One of the things that I personally utilize is a money market account.

This is essentially a savings account that is invested for you. There are a variety of companies that you can go with; I would personally suggest using Fidelity or Vanguard. They seem to be the top dogs in these areas and the most reliable. I think one of the fears of people who have never invested before is that they think they can lose all their money if they do not invest it in the right things. That is true, but not with money market accounts. It is virtually impossible for them to ever lose money, and they are federally insured.

It is really set up like a savings account. You can withdraw and deposit money as you wish with no penalties, and the more money you have in this account, the more money you make. They'll send you a statement every month or every quarter, so you can actually see how much extra money you're making.

There are also a variety of high(er) interest earning checking/savings accounts available out there that you just need to go out and find. Without going into too much detail, you're just looking for a place to park your money, while still having complete access to it, that is one hundred percent free to do. So, if you go the route of a checking/savings account, make sure they are not sticking you with any kind of fees at all.

And you can do all of this yourself, without consulting a financial advisor or specialist. If you have noticed, not once have I advised you to consult a specialist in this book. This is because I always hated reading this when I was looking for advice on a particular subject. I didn't research something on the Internet or in a book only to be told by someone to call or ask someone else—heck, that's why I was doing the research in the first place!

Now obviously, I do not have ALL of the answers in this book, but in this particular instance, I know that you can do all of it yourself. Research it a little on the Internet, maybe call the company that you are interested in with any further questions, and set it up yourself. No need at all for financial advisors or specialists or anything like that. Know why? Because I'd say it's a pretty good bet that they cost money!

Credit cards—And finally, a few notes about credit cards in general. The best thing I can tell you on top of everything else that I have already told you is that the best attribute that you want in your credit card is the ability to get CASH BACK. I have never ever been a big believer in Delta Sky Miles or a GM card or anything else. Now, this opinion may be slightly out of ignorance, but I can tell you this much. With respect to the more generic credit cards that only have the reward programs where you can choose gifts and what not, you would still want to go with one with a cash back option.

The reason that I say this is that what you need to have more of in your life is money, not stuff.

Plus, money is your most valuable option with these cards. You can do far more with the cash that they offer you than any of the gifts or anything else that they offer. And think about it, most of the time, if you choose one of the gifts or material things that they offer, aren't you really getting something that you don't truly want or don't truly need? That's exactly how I feel. Give me the cash and I'll buy what I want or put it towards my balance.

This next section is only for advanced users I guess you could say.

There is a way that you can generate a good deal of money through the use of credit cards without spending a dime. The only thing that you will need is a great deal of organization. Because if you don't stay organized, you can really kind of screw yourself. Not to the point of losing money, but you could lose everything you made if you're not careful.

I actually thought I discovered this little trick on my own, until I later found out that lots of people have done it and still do it.

The name they came up with for it is called "app-o-rama."

I never had a name for it; I just did it to make some easy money.

First and foremost, you must have excellent credit history to do it, and again you must be organized.

Now, I am currently doing this on a much bigger scale, but here is how one would begin. I'll actually explain exactly what I am doing at the end. Again, not to beat a dead horse, you need to have great credit and be quite disciplined.

What you would do is to find a credit card you could sign up for that offers a 0% APR (including balance transfers, that is very important) for as long a period of time as you can find, hopefully at least one year. Sign up for it. These cards are a little more difficult to find than they used to be, so if you can't find that, find the next closest thing. The one I used the last time offered that but the balance transfer option had a fee of $75 that went along with it. Don't worry; I made my $75 back in the first month. Anyways, sign up for it and say you get your limit of $4,000 (this is not out of the question if your credit is very good).

Then, you call them up and tell them you want to exercise the balance transfer option. Before, most of the credit card companies out there would do this for you, but they would only send the check in the name of a creditor. For some reason, some or most of them have switched this policy and now will send a check made out to you if you request it. This is the key. You definitely want to tell them that you want the full amount, and that you want it in the form of a check made out to you.

If all goes well, you should have this $4,000 arriving at your doorstep in a few weeks. Now, here is where the discipline and organization and all that comes in. You do not need to spend this money! Remember, the point of this whole venture is for you to generate income, not waste it. What you need to do is to invest it in a money market account (hopefully, one that you have already opened).

Of course, you will still get a monthly bill from the credit card company. Here is where the organization comes in. You cannot miss a payment with this credit card. You cannot miss a payment, you cannot be late with a payment, and also, you want to cut up this credit card as soon as you receive it, because you definitely do not ever want to put any purchases on it.

What you want to do is to make your minimum monthly payment on the card every month until the end of the term of the promotional rate. Make the payment out of your own savings, or if you are not yet in that position, just withdraw enough out of your money market to make the monthly payment. Then, you just sit back and wait. Wait and watch this money make money for you. Then of course, you just send all the money back right before the promotional term ends.

But again, I cannot emphasize enough the importance of:

1) NOT SPENDING THE MONEY
2) MAKING ALL MONTHLY PAYMENTS ON TIME AND IN FULL
3) NOT FORGETTING TO PAY OFF THE BALANCE BEFORE THE PROMOTIONAL TERM ENDS.

Failure to do any of these will probably void the promotional rate and sometimes the credit card company will charge you all of the interest that you would have owed since you first had the card. That's a little bit of a scary thought, but as long as you are disciplined and organized, you should not have a problem. I have been doing this every year for four years now and I have never missed a payment.

A very rough generalized estimate on what you can make over the course of a year with $4,000 invested in a money market account is right around $325. Free and clear. Pretty nice. Of course, this does also depend greatly on exactly where you put your money. Obviously, the results will vary.

I am currently up to amounts much higher than that. What I do is to always open up a credit card by the same company with whom I have another credit card with that has a very large limit on it. I open up the new one and go through the whole process. The only difference is that before I do I tell them I want to consolidate my new card with my other card with the high spending limit on it and then I request my balance transfer. I won't get into specific numbers, but let's just say I have been able to generate a great deal of income for myself over these past four years.

A side note—lately, the credit card companies have made this "app-o-rama" thing close to impossible, but I have also heard that with competition between credit card companies the way that it is, that the "app-o-rama" may be making a comeback some day soon.

Finally, a great way to try to begin to generate income in your own life is to start a project in your spare time. By "project" I do not mean painting the house or reorganizing a closet. I mean a project similar to what I did with this book.

I spoke about it earlier, but you should seriously consider it! What you first need to do is to identify one of your talents or passions. For me, one of my passions and talents is writing. Also, I think one of my talents is saving money. One day, it just hit me. Of course, I think it had something to do with the economy. I think it also had to do with the increased amount of advice I was giving out for friends and family on different ways to save money.

I combined the two, and believe it or not, I wrote this book in my spare time. I maintained my full time job the whole time, and I just did it. Mostly before I went to work in the morning, a little bit here and there, and five or six months later, I had myself a book.

Of course, your talent may not be writing or saving money.

But you know what? EVERYBODY, and I mean everybody has a talent. What you need to do is figure out how to transfer this into something that can generate money for you.

With a lot of this information, I am getting into things that I am not an expert at, but I know people who are.

Let me give you an overview and then explain.

Say, for example, you have a talent at woodworking or carpentry. You happen to be really good at it. Let's say that you have a lot of generalized tips that most beginning "woodworkers" so to speak may not know, and that you think might be able to add value to these peoples' lives (or at least to their hobbies).

That's the first thing you're looking for—the ability to add value. Again, it goes back to your talent. Everybody in this world does something well. Find what your talent is and find how you can add value to other peoples' lives who want to learn your skill.

Then, maybe you write an e-book on the subject. An e-book is really just a short book. Maybe ten, fifteen, twenty, or even thirty pages. Say you write this e-book on *Tips for Beginning Carpenters*. Then, you just have to promote your e-book and get people to pay you a small sum of money for this e-book.

This is really just a small, crude example of what one could possibly do to generate income without picking up a second job or anything like that.

I am oversimplifying the process, but this is basically how it goes. In keeping with one of the re-occurring themes in this book, it has a lot to do with your mental outlook. Find your passion, act on it, don't ever give up. It's simple.

Another thing that I recently did that helps me generate more money is that I signed up all of my utility bills to be paid by credit card. Why, you ask? Well, I signed them up on my card that gives me 1% cash back on my purchases. If you add up my utilities for a month and multiply it times twelve (that pesky "times twelve" rule again) I generated almost an extra $100 a year for myself. Do you know how long it took to set all of that up? About an hour or so.

In conclusion, think hard about identifying your own talents and how to translate that into a money-making opportunity, and discover the power of the Internet and how it can also be utilized as a tool for generating income, whether by selling items there, or uncovering research or deals or coupons that will allow you to save yourself some money.

CHAPTER 6

Credit Rating

"Remember that credit is money."

- Benjamin Franklin

In this day and age, from what I can understand, your credit rating can now have an effect on everything from how much you pay in auto insurance to your ability to get a job, to your ability to get a date this Friday night. Well, I am exaggerating about the date part, but who knows?

Your credit rating is important. You should know what it is, and where you can get it without paying money for it. More importantly, you should know how to get it as high as possible, and it if is already good, you should know what you need to do to keep it there. So here we go...

Paying bills on time

As I was finally gaining some momentum in my quest to be rid of financial stress, I had been hearing over and over again that paying your bills on time goes a long way in many areas. Have a desire to buy a house? Pay your bills on time for at least six months prior. Want to raise your credit score? Pay your bills on time. Want to get a low rate of interest on a car loan or other type of loan? Again, pay your bills on time.

I also heard recently that your ability to pay your bills on time makes up approximately thirty percent of your credit score. The rest of it is broken down as follows. There is another thirty percent which is the amount of debt you have with respect to the amount of overall credit you have (meaning, you want to have as much open credit as possible available to you). The last thirty percent or so is made up of your history (the longer the better, the frequency with which you apply for new credit, and the types of credit that you have). To me, the biggest impact that you can have on your credit score is simple—pay your bills on time. If one of your bills does not get paid on time but it is not your fault, contact the company and make sure that it is fixed, immediately!

Another smaller way to increase your score is to open more lines of credit if you are able to. Open up a few extra cards with a decent-sized limit on them. This should improve your score too. Just make sure to use the card every so often. Credit card companies are now identifying these so-called "dormant" cards and either closing them or reducing the limit. Also, make sure to keep them in a safe place when not in use. If you are only using a certain card once every three months, there is no need to carry it in your wallet or purse.

Fixing credit history

As I have already mentioned briefly, a good credit score/history will be a necessity for you at some point in your life. It probably helps you out in many more ways than you think. These days, your credit report is accessed for just about everything you can think of. As I said, it can now play a part in whether a certain job is offered to you (prospective employers are now known to check credit histories along with criminal backgrounds). It can also affect things like auto insurance rates. The overall "fixing" of your credit score (if it needs fixing) should, in a lot of ways, simply take care of itself. Not to sound like a broken record, but paying your bills in a timely manner on a consistent basis goes a long way to raising your credit score. Just by doing this you should be able to put your credit score almost where it needs to be. However, there is also another step that I began taking about four to five years ago which I would also suggest you do. First, when you begin to get serious about fixing your entire financial situation, I would request and get a free copy of your credit report. Let me emphasize the word "free." There are probably about a million Web sites out there that will provide you with your credit report for a fee, and as far as I have been able to gather, only about two or three that will actually do it for free. Guess where I am going to direct you? Of course! To the free ones. One place to go is:

www.annualcreditreport.com

Here, you can get your credit report from each of the three reporting companies once a year for free.

Also, I think you can get your credit score whenever you want for free at the "E-loan" Web site. It might re-direct you to...

www.creditkarma.com

Either way, these sites offer a way to get your report free, one time a year or more. If worse comes to worse, go to one of the pay sites, sign up, get your free report and cancel your subscription before the thirty days is up so your credit card is not charged.

The reason I suggest getting your report to begin with is that there could be errors on your report that are negatively affecting your score. I have yet to have this problem and have never had to go through the process of getting something "fixed" on my credit report, but I have heard that it is not that easy. Actually I believe it is easier than it used to be, but still not a lot of fun. Additionally, ordering and reviewing your credit report at least once a year will also keep you on top of things such as preventing potential identity theft.

What I would suggest doing is reading your credit report and looking for any negative things on it that don't belong there. Another thing depends upon which agency you get your report from (Equifax, Trans Union, and Experian). They are not the easiest things to read, but you should be able to fish your way through it for the most part. The problem is that it lists your entire credit history! When I first looked at mine, I was a little shocked, because it had everything on there all the way down to a Burdines's credit card that I got and never used more than twenty years ago. The first step is to analyze your report for any errors and if there are any, to get them fixed or taken off.

Here is what I would do in a nutshell:

1) ORDER YOUR CREDIT REPORTS, AT LEAST ONCE A YEAR.

2) READ AND EXAMINE THEM, AND TAKE ACTION IF NEED BE. IF THERE IS BAD HISTORY BECAUSE OF YOUR OWN ACTIONS, THE ONLY THING THAT CAN CHANGE IT IS TIME AND IMPROVING YOUR HABITS. BUT IF YOU'VE COME THIS FAR IN THIS BOOK YOU SHOULD BE WELL ON YOUR WAY.

3) TAKE METICULOUS NOTES AND LOOK AT EVERYTHING. EVEN CHECK FOR TYPOGRAPHICAL ERRORS!

4) WITH ANY AND ALL ERRORS, EITHER COMPLETE THE DISPUTE FORM OR WRITE THE REPORTING AGENCY A SEPARATE LETTER. CLEARLY IDENTIFY EACH ITEM THAT YOU ARE DISPUTING (I WOULD SUGGEST MAKING A COPY OF THE REPORT ITSELF AND CIRCLING ALL DISPUTED ITEMS).

5) DOCUMENT, DOCUMENT, DOCUMENT. KEEP METICULOUS, ORGANIZED AND COMPLETE DOCUMENTATION TO EVERYTHING YOU SEND IN TO THE REPORTING AGENCIES. THEY ARE REQUIRED TO RESPOND TO ANY VALID DISPUTE WITHIN THIRTY DAYS, AND IF THEY CANNOT VERIFY THE VALIDITY OF THE ISSUE IN DISPUTE, THEN IT MUST BE REMOVED FROM YOUR REPORT. THEN, THEY MUST SEND YOU AN UPDATED, FREE COPY OF YOUR NEW REPORT WITH YOUR NEW SCORE.

6) FINALLY, IF THERE ARE ANY ISSUES WHICH THE REPORTING AGENCY TELLS YOU THAT YOU NEED TO CONTACT THE CREDITOR DIRECTLY, THAT'S FINE. BUT BEFORE YOU DO, PLEASE RE-READ MY SECTION ON DISPUTES AND HOW TO WIN THEM. YOU BASICALLY NEED TO APPLY ALL OF THE ADVICE THAT I GIVE IN THAT SECTION TO THIS PARTICULAR AREA. SOMETIMES, IT COULD JUST BE A MATTER OF A FEW PHONE CALLS; OTHER TIMES, IT MAY REQUIRE YOU TO STAND UP AND FIGHT.

And that is my two cents on your credit rating. If you need further information on a specific topic, research the Internet or contact the "money" person that you should have in your life by now. I discuss this and a few other people that you need to have in your life in Chapter 8. At least I didn't direct you to a financial advisor, right?

CHAPTER 7

Taxes

*The only difference between a tax man and a taxidermist is
that the taxidermist leaves the skin.*
- Mark Twain

This chapter can essentially be summed up in three words...

...DO IT YOURSELF...

Have you been taking your taxes to an accountant, or even
worse (much much worse) one of those walk-in tax places like
H & R Block or Jackson Hewitt? Unless you own your own
business or your current tax situation is so confusing that it
really does require a professional, the first and best piece of
advice that I can give you is to *do it yourself*. Besides one year,
when I wasted $300, I have never paid anyone to do my taxes.
To date, I have never made a mistake, I have never been audited

and I have yet to have one problem. And as I have already stated many other times in many other places, I am just a regular guy. I promise that you can figure this out.

Up until the time that I purchased my first home, I even did it without any tax software. At that point in time, I really didn't have any investments to speak of, no other real tax considerations, and it was just a matter of filling out the EZ form and sending it in. I would imagine that most of you over the age of twenty-five have situations a little more complicated than this, but I am only using this as an example. Doing your own taxes is not that difficult. Of course, sending in a paper copy of your return will mean that your refund does not come as fast, but we'll get to that point a little later.

For those of you who cannot completely do it on your own, this is one time where I will actually recommend spending some money. I have purchased tax software for probably about the last six years. I personally use Tax Cut, but there are many others out there. I like Tax Cut because it is virtually idiot-proof. It will ask you questions in a so-called "interview" about your finances for the past year, and then it is really just step-by-step through the process until you're done. It even asks you questions to make sure you don't miss any deductions or credits and offers ways to be able to take a specific credit or deduction by doing certain things. Best of all, the cost of purchasing the tax software itself is also tax-deductible.

I know that you can probably get most forms from the IRS Web site and you might be able to do your taxes no matter how complicated without purchasing any software, but e-filing your taxes through the software you buy speeds up your return, and although I have never used it, I doubt that doing your taxes from the IRS Web site is as simple and easy as buying software. I imagine you would need to have a better technical understanding of your finances to do it this way. So, put simply, buying software is a good investment, it is completely doable by anyone that is remotely intelligent, the cost of the software is tax deductible, and depending on which version you buy, they do offer free support in case you are ever audited. Just research the different versions well, as they will try to sell you the Deluxe, most expensive package, when you may be able to get by with a cheaper one.

IF THAT'S SIMPLY NOT AN OPTION, DO NOT TAKE YOUR MONEY EARLY! DON'T BE A MULE!

If everything that I outlined above is simply not an option, I do have some advice for you. I don't know, maybe you are simply too intimidated by it all, maybe too afraid of making a mistake, I am not sure and I am not here to judge. If there is no other option for you other than to take it to one of those walk-in places and have them do it—DO NOT TAKE YOUR MONEY EARLY! I hear it all the time from people that use those services and almost all of them choose whatever rip-off option it is that they offer, but they all take their money early. I don't even want to know how much they shave off of your return but I am quite sure it is not cheap. This is where changing your attitudes and beliefs towards money also plays a big role.

Let's begin by saying this—this tax returrn money is YOUR money. It is not some gift from the government or anything else. You have worked just as hard throughout the year for this tax return money as you did for all the money that showed up on your paychecks; you need to treat it that way. That is the only guess that I can fathom as to why people almost always use this option and give away their own money.

Because they look at it as money that wasn't theirs in the first place.

Or something along those lines. I honestly have no idea. Anyways, do not take it early. Show a little patience and get ALL of your money back. I know that when I use my software, my federal return money normally appears within about two weeks. So the wait is not that bad. No matter how long these people tell you the wait will be, just suck it up and wait. I have another un-thought-of point that most people don't realize.

You have waited the entire year for this money anyways—what's a few more extra days going to hurt?

For those of you who owe taxes on a consistent basis we can later take a look at some ways to change this, but for now, I would only advise that you wait till the last minute to file. Again, it is your money—just because you have to give some back to the government does not mean you have to give it back any earlier than necessary.

If you have decided to make the change and start doing your taxes yourself, or even if you are currently doing them on your own, the following is a good set of guidelines to ensure that you are maximizing your return and that you are doing it in the most organized and feasible way possible.

BEGIN A SIMPLE FILING SYSTEM

Here is where we begin to do a little planning and organization that will set you up for some long-term success come tax time. Of course, some of these steps you may not be able to implement in time for any substantial savings in your current tax year, but that's OK. We can at least set ourselves up for the future. And with some of these things you might still be able to get some of the benefit this year. It really just depends on your record-keeping system that you have in place right now (if any) and your ability to use the Internet to obtain your bill information from throughout the year.

What you need to do is to begin a simple filing system. This step will lead into one of my other steps (itemizing), which we will get to in a minute. I personally have a small filing cabinet next to my computer that I use for all of my documents. Whatever works for you. What I do personally is that I save all of my utility bills throughout the year in separate files, and I also save all of my credit card statements throughout the year. Will your utility bills ever really come into play with regard to doing your taxes? No. But I can assure you that they are worth holding onto, at least for one year. You may need them for a loan application, or more importantly, if you ever have a dispute with your utility company.

With my credit card statements, I highlight on each one whatever charge may be a potential credit or deduction, or anything tax-related, and that goes into a file called "Taxes." This makes things much easier at the end of the year. As with anything else, I will tell you that before I instituted this filing system, I had always thought that it would be a waste of time, too much to keep track of, take too much time, etc. Well, after I set it up, and after I got used to it, which took all of about one month, it is now a habit of mine that takes zero time out of my days to keep up with.

More importantly is your mindset towards doing your taxes. Your income taxes represent a way in which you can do all three things that I advocate to put people on the road to financial freedom—you can spend less money, you can save more money, and you can generate more income. All with just a little planning. This is the question that I pose to you: When do you need to start planning for your taxes? For example, take your 2007 tax return. When did you start working on it? January 1, 2008? Later than that? Whenever you got your W-2? OK, those would be wrong, wrong, and wrong. The time to begin planning for that particular return would have been January 1, 2007! Yes, really! When I was first told this, I thought it was a crazy idea, I thought there was no way that I could even think about my taxes throughout and so on. Now, it is by force of habit. I do it without even actually thinking about it.

We can't go back in time, but you can start planning for your next year's taxes right now. So many things happen throughout the year financially that have an effect on your taxes that you will never remember them all and unless you have a filing system—something will fall through the cracks. We have already outlined what this filing system needs to have in it, and I promise you, it is not complicated. Virtually nothing that I offer anywhere in this book is complicated or difficult to do.

Another way to simplify the process is to pay for as many things as you can with a credit card. That way, you do not have to ask for receipts for every little thing and then keep track of these receipts; all the information you will need arrives monthly on your credit card statement. However, if you do not carry a $0 balance on your credit cards, this may not make financial sense. If possible, reserve one card that you can pay down to $0 every month, and use that for all of your purchases, etc. that are going to be tax deductible.

Again, this may sound like a lot, but the hardest part is implementing this system and trying to stick to it. Once it becomes a habit, it is amazingly easy.

If you want to try to begin to reap the benefits of this system for this year's taxes, simply finish reading my other steps, and then try to access as many records as you can from the Internet. The "biggies" to try to get would be your credit card statements for the year, and the amount you paid for health insurance premiums. Most bill statements and credit card statements are available and saved on the Internet.

As I stated just now, there are many reasons to keep track of your credit card statements and utility bill statements throughout the year. In addition to what I just mentioned, keeping these records may also assist you in the following:

–Apply for a student loan for you or a member of your family.

–Refinance your home

–Apply for your first mortgage, or any kind of loan.

–Have any kind if issues with immigration and naturalization (for those of us who are not yet citizens)

–Most importantly, if you ever have an item paid for by credit card that you want to dispute.

So do yourself a favor and expand your filing system to include your bills and all your credit card statements. I can almost assure you that something is going to happen to you someday that is going to make you happy that you did this. Plus, after you have filed your taxes and you basically close the book on that particular tax year—just empty out all the files, hold onto any tax-related documents, shred the rest, and start over.

ACCURACY IN RECORDS

Do you know how many errors occur on tax returns because of simple errors?? A lot more than you might think. If you do make an error on your tax return and realize it after it has been filed, there is a way to correct it, but it is not very easy. It is much easier to focus on accuracy from the beginning. First, focus on accuracy when filing your return. This applies whether you file on paper or with software. I would venture to say more importantly if you file electronically, because it is much easier to punch in a wrong number on a keyboard than it is to actually write down a wrong number incorrectly on a paper return. Accuracy is important! Before filing your return, double-check it (triple check it if necessary) and verify your entries!

Personally, it takes me probably one week altogether to prepare my return each year. Of course, this is not one actual week of work, just one week from the time I start until the time I finish. The actual work time is probably about three hours. It is only three hours because I have all of my numbers just waiting to be inputted. It is probably between one to two hours to input the numbers the first time around. Then I go back and double-check everything for accuracy. And then, just to be sure, I put my taxes aside for about one week, and basically try to not to think about them. Actually, the only thing that I do think about is if there was anything that I forgot to include from my files or anything else. This has become a very profitable week for me in the past because usually, there is something that I forgot or there is something in the return itself that I realized that I did not do correctly. To me, this week is very important. After about one week, I go back to my return and I check it one more time from beginning to end. This gives me the peace of mind that I have done everything correctly and I have not left anything out.

Finally, even though I pay for EVERYTHING with a credit card, I also try to keep the receipt for anything that is not obvious what it is. And, I DEFINITELY keep the receipt also for anything that I know is going to be a larger deduction or credit. For example, if I lose a receipt for $6 worth of dry cleaning, it is probably not a big deal, because I will have the name of the dry cleaner on my credit card statement, and I will also have twenty other receipts from them throughout the year. However, if I buy a home computer over the Internet and it shows up on my bill as "ACME Delivery" or something that I might forget, I have the receipt for the computer as a back-up. Plus, you would want to keep the receipt for that anyway.

ITEMIZE YOUR DEDUCTIONS

Here is a "biggie." In the past, I always did my taxes the easiest way possible—filing by paper with the EZ form, taking the standard deduction and sending it in. Well, for most of us, and ESPECIALLY for those of us who either just bought a home or bought one in the past five years, in my opinion, you definitely want to itemize your deductions. I cannot remember exactly what the difference was, but the first year I itemized my deductions, I think the standard deduction was around $10,000 and by the time I was finished I had over $16,000 in deductions. This represented a HUGE tax savings, a larger tax return check, and it did not take that much more time. Even if it did take a lot more time, it was well worth the money. The first year that you itemize, the process of doing your taxes is probably going to be time-consuming. However, with each year it becomes easier and a more efficient process.

Itemizing my deductions proved to be more profitable for me even before any of the following happened to me:

—getting married
—having children
—buying a home
—investing

For those of you that think that you need one of these life-changing events in your life to make it worthwhile itemizing, I think that would be an incorrect assumption. If you implement the filing system we spoke about above, if you begin thinking about your taxes not at the end of the year but throughout the year, and you keep good records, you can get more of your hard-earned money back from the government than you might ever have imagined.

JREs

Here, we begin to go over some of the files that you will need to establish and maintain throughout the year in order to impact your tax savings. The reason for starting this file at the beginning of the year is to get the thought in your mind some of the things that are tax deductible throughout the year, and to also be able to do a lot of the legwork for your tax return throughout the year rather than all at the end of the year. I simply have a file in my filing cabinet with "JRE" written at the top, and at the end of the year, I create a document (Word or spreadsheet) and transpose all of the info onto one form with a total at the bottom. You can maintain this document throughout the year if you'd like. I find it simpler to do it at the end of the year.

A JRE, in my simplistic terminology, stands for **Job-Related Expense**. You may not think that many items would fall under this category, but allow me to explain. Most of the expenses in this category for me are dry cleaning expenses and uniforms for work (the expense of a tie or a dress shirt that is only worn to work *is* deductible). Let's move on to some things you may not know are deductible. For anyone in your home who has started a new business, there is a large list of things that are deductible. You would have to utilize your tax software to know the specifics, but if you have created a home office used for the purposes of business, chances are a lot of those expenses are deductible. If you use a vehicle for this business (or even the vehicle that you yourself use to get back and forth to work at your regular job) there are deductions here that can be taken advantage of.

A lot of meals can be deducted as business expenses if they qualify. If you take one of your co-workers out to lunch and business is discussed at this lunch, more than likely it is deductible. If you rarely eat out, it may not be worth the trouble to keep track of the receipt and to file it correctly and to remember that a lunch that you paid $10 for last January is deductible when almost a year has gone by. However, if you do eat out a lot, if you do incur expenses that are not reimbursed by your employer for things you buy for your job, and the other things that I mentioned above, this CAN add up to some substantial savings for you.

Basically, I save all my credit card statements that have the "no-brainers" on them. That is, the dry-cleaning stuff, the uniforms and so on. Then, if there is anything else that I think has a remote chance of being deductible, I throw it in my JRE file with a fairly detailed note of what it is, and I wait until I go through the interview with my tax software to see if it is something I can deduct. Remember, and I will be clear on this, you do not want to deduct anything that is clearly non-deductible, and you do not want to do anything fraudulent or unethical when filing your taxes. The only thing that I am trying to show you here is that you can get back more of your hard-earned money from the government through some prudent record-keeping throughout the year.

UMEs

The second category that I have in my filing system for my taxes is titled "UMEs". This stands for **Un-reimbursed Medical Expenses**. As I am sure you have now figured out, money that you spend on medical expenses for you or your family that is not reimbursed by your insurance carrier is tax deductible. The most important year that this category will come into play would be the first year after the birth of a child. I never realized that all these expenses were tax deductible, and I never realized that in the year directly following the birth of a child, there would be so many—especially if you do not have the greatest health plan in the world, or if you do not have health insurance at all.

I actually fell into the first category (not a great health plan) several years ago when my son was born, and the deductions and resulting tax savings were tremendous. I believe I had around $6,000 in this category, so you can imagine what I saved (or how much more I got back) on my taxes. It tends to go down somewhat in the years following, but it is highly worth the time that it takes to keep up with your medical bills throughout the year. Again, consider utilizing a credit card for these charges—this goes a long way in helping you stay organized throughout the year.

Additionally, there is something that I did not realize until even a few years after I started doing my own taxes. This point goes to show you that you can always continue to learn and can always impact your tax burden because the tax laws are always changing. And depending upon who's in the White House, some tax law changes can even benefit us the taxpayer! It was just a few years ago that I found out (with a little research) that the health insurance premiums that you pay throughout the year, in *some* circumstances, are tax deductible. Again, you would have to follow along the interview with your tax software but this can also represent tremendous savings at tax time.

Because for most of us, what we pay out-of-pocket throughout the year for health insurance it still a fairly large amount (so it may benefit you to keep all of your paystubs from work in a separate file also).

There are some things that do not fall into this category that you should be aware of. But again, follow closely along in your interview with your tax software to find out for sure. Over-the-counter medicines are not tax deductible. I personally think that they should be, but they are not. Remember, you always want to stay "above board" when doing your taxes. Whenever I am in doubt about something, I usually do not write it off. But you do want to get everything that is rightfully yours.

Once again, this category can represent huge savings for you if you recently had a child or if you spend a lot of money on health-related issues throughout the year that are not reimbursed by your insurance carrier. It is well worth the time to keep up with this over the course of a year.

JSEs

This category, depending upon your situation, could mean some very good savings for you, then again it might not. But it is worth keeping up with. This JSE category stands for **Job Search Expenses**. And that is exactly what it means. Money that you spend throughout the year looking for a new job is tax deductible. Your savings here depends on your situation. Several years ago, it represented a fairly decent amount of savings for me, because during one tax year I had utilized the services of one of those "head-hunter" companies that supposedly goes out and finds you a job. I realized after the fact that it was probably money not very well spent, but I learned a lot and I got to write off the money I spent. But even if you do not take that step and you are in the hunt for a new job, think hard about some of the things that can fall under this category:

—clothes for job interviews (suits, dresses, etc.)
—resume preparation fees
—postage for resume mail-outs
—printing supplies for resumes
—gasoline used going to/from job interviews
—memberships to employment Web sites

And there are probably a few other things that can be added to the list that I am not thinking of at the moment. Just remember, keep good, accurate records, and if you were in, or are planning to be in the hunt for a new job, the expenses that you incur during this hunt are tax deductible.

DONATE/CHARITABLE CONTRIBUTIONS

Here is another area that I have taken advantage of fully in the past few years. All donations/charitable contributions made to a qualifying organization are tax deductible. As far as the definition of a "qualifying organization" it basically means that it can't be a person, and it basically means that it is a church or a religious organization or something like Goodwill. Once again, I found the exact definition of this on the software I used for my taxes.

Any money that you donate to a church/religious organization throughout the year is tax deductible. And this category also happens to be what I call a "feel good" category because any time you do anything in this category, in addition to the tax savings, you also are doing something that makes you feel good inside. So the benefit is really double. When donating to your church, however, I would either donate by check, or be sure that your church will be able to provide you with a statement at the end of the year detailing your amounts donated. The former is sometimes easier—churches I have dealt with in the past seem to have struggled with their record-keeping. But keep in mind that the money is tax deductible. One additional idea is to simply make one big donation at the beginning or the end of the tax year to minimize the record-keeping, but most of us seem to do better budgeting it on a weekly/monthly basis.

With respect to charitable contributions, I want to make a side note first. I am a firm non-believer in garage sales. I dislike having them, for two reasons (shopping at them is a different story—I have no problem with shopping at them). I dislike having them because they are very time-consuming and also because no matter how inexpensive you mark your items, you will always get the majority of people there asking to pay even less. This always drove me nuts at any garage sale I was a part of. Third, I think that you can impact your tax savings even more by simply donating your items and writing off their worth.

Now, as far as how to do it, this is what I do. For any larger items such as big household furniture and/or appliances, not all qualifying organizations pick these things up (I think that the National Kidney Foundation will still come to your house for them). Simply contact your local chapter and ask to be sure. For everything else, just pick someone and get involved with them, and pretty soon, they should be calling your house every few months to see if you have anything for them, so you don't even have to remember anything. What you do have to remember is to make a good notation of whatever you donate, and make sure to value it fairly (now, the value of these items is not going to be very much, but think about it...how much would you have gotten for it had you sold it a garage sale anyways?) You basically need to value it at "thrift shop" value, and most tax software will even include a "valuator" of some sort to assist you with how much some particular item is worth.

About once every three months, I go through all of my closets and if I have not worn something in the past six months (referring to clothing) or I have not used something in the past three months (referring to everything else except items used seasonally). I think hard about whether or not I really need it. If it is in good enough condition, there are ways to get more money for it, but most of the time I just bag it up and donate it. Just recently I even found a drop-off center for Goodwill that is about three minutes from my house. Now I don't even save stuff up for a few months. I found that when doing this, you are more likely to change your mind and hold on to something that you don't really use any more or don't really need any more. Do yourself a favor—donate the item, make a good record of it, valuate it fairly, help keep your closets from overflowing and best of all, make a person needier than yourself quite happy.

401K

Here is my tenth and final easy way to save money on your taxes, and save money in general. It is called a 401K and it is offered by most employers. I am mentioning this again because I want to emphasize its importance as a savings tool. The benefits to enrolling in this are far too many to detail here. Put briefly, you can elect to have a certain dollar amount taken out of your paycheck each week or a percentage of your pay. Let's say for example, you decide on $20 per week, which would probably be a good amount if you're just starting out, not quite set financially, or don't understand the process yet. Depending on your employer, you can bump it up or down virtually whenever you want to. So, $20 is taken out of your check each week. The first benefit is that this money is taken out before the government takes taxes out of your check, so you do not pay taxes on this $20. The next benefit is that the money does not just sit somewhere collecting dust, it is put in an investment account (the particular investments are chosen by you) and with any luck, it should begin to gain interest as well. If you need help with which investment(s) to choose, see the section coming up about the three people that you need to have in your life to be financially successful. If you still don't have a "financial" guy, ask around work, you're liable to find somebody you trust who can at least point you in the right direction. The third benefit is that most employers offer what they call a "match." Meaning, they contribute money to your account just because you are contributing. Some offer a one hundred percent match, meaning that your $20 will actually be $40 after your employer match; with other companies the matching percentage is a little less.

These are three obvious benefits of beginning a 401K program. The benefit I like the best is that this is money that you really never "see," if you get my point, and it is the perfect way to save money for those of us who have difficulty saving. It is taken out automatically, you don't have to do anything, and over the course of a year, it really adds up. After the first few weeks of having a little less in your paycheck, you really don't notice it and if you find that you can afford to do more, go ahead and bump it up. Just keep in mind that you cannot touch this money before retirement without significant penalties.

And there you have it, the majority of my expertise on the subject of taxes. As with most everything else in this book, I learned all of what you just read on my own, mostly through experience. This is just another testament to how I *know* that the material contained in this book actually works. It is not just some theory that I invented, it is stuff that I learned or came up with over the years, and it all works and there are significant benefits to all of it. I know that if you have gotten this far in this book that you probably don't need to hear this right now, but it bears repeating. Everything contained in this book was written out of the life experiences of myself. I was further in debt than most people have ever been, and considering the money I currently make, I am as financially sound as I could ever hope to be.

CHAPTER 8

Closing and Final Notes, and the Surprise Ending

"It's good to have money and the things that money can buy, but it's good, too, to check up once in a while and make sure that you haven't lost the things that money can't buy." - George Lorimer

Over these past years of going from the depths of financial hell to the moderate successes that I am currently enjoying, I certainly would never be so arrogant to say that I did it all on my own. I will say that through most of it, I knew which questions to ask which people, and I also had the luxury of having a few key people in my life whom I relied upon for a good bit of the advice and help that I received. Here are those people in a nutshell:

A finance person. When I first got serious about all of this, I did have one person in my life that I considered to be a money/finance/investing expert. That person is my mother. I had someone in my life that I trusted and who knew quite a bit about the areas I just mentioned. Maybe that person will turn out to be me for a lot of you. If not, it needs to be someone. You need to have someone in your life who you can ask questions of, get advice from, etc. Once you get going on this personal finance stuff, you will come up with ways to save money on your own. But in the beginning, you'll probably want a guide. You may already have one in your life; you just don't know it yet. Find out a little more about the people in your "contact list" and you can probably find someone. I would seek out the help of a professional financial advisor only as a last resort; I despise most of them with a passion only because they are mostly just out to sell you things. Remember, the point here is to try to save money, not spend more unnecessarily.

A good insurance person. Think about it. What kind of insurance do most of us currently have? The biggies are health, home owners/renter's, auto, life, and then there are a variety of others. That's a lot of insurance. Now, for most of us, health insurance is mostly a non-issue, because our coverage is through whoever our employer uses. But for some of us who have private health insurance, there could be some room there to save money. With regards to all the other types of insurance, trust me, you can easily impact your wallet. It seems to me that these are some areas that one may not realize at first that you can save money. I say this because your home owner's insurance bill is usually wrapped into your mortgage payment, so you really don't even pay this bill, and with life insurance, I always assumed that everything was about the same. This is a perfect example of the saying, *"It's not what you know, it's who you know."* The best advice I can give you for finding a person like this is to choose an independent agent. These are the people who basically work for themselves, and who are not really associated with any one particular company. Therefore, they don't really care who your insurance is bought through. So, they will obviously do their best to see that you both have the best insurance that you need and the cheapest. I personally have used the same insurance agent for the past twelve years, and she has been able to save me a lot of money, in a lot of different areas. Also, concerning insurance, consider purchasing different types of policies from the same company for an added discount. Try wrapping your auto, home owner's, and life insurance altogether and your company should offer you a pretty decent discount.

A mortgage guy. With everything that has gone on of late, I am sure you know that there are a lot of less-than-ethical people in this industry—making it even more important to have someone you can trust. There are so many bad mortgages out there, so much "crap" out there, that having someone you can trust can give you the peace of mind of knowing that you have the best and least expensive mortgage out there. The person that I know in this field I have known for over ten years, he has refinanced my house three times for me, and I would actually consider him a personal friend now, that's how close we have become. If you don't currently have this person in your life, I would consider a referral rather than seeking out someone "cold." Speak with your friends and co-workers and find someone they trust. Another reason why I mention having this type of person in your life is because typically, if you develop a good relationship with them, they can also offer good advice in other areas related to mortgages (i.e., real estate, real estate agents, some types of lawyers, home inspectors, the list goes on).

A Computer guy. I'd like to think that over the years I have become pretty proficient at fixing minor problems with computers and also learning different software applications. I never really took any courses, most of the stuff I basically taught myself.

Having said this, I still consider myself in great need of a "computer guy." What I mean by this is a person that can explain to you how to do something in Microsoft Word if you need it and you don't know how to do it yourself, someone who can get something to stop appearing on your screen whenever you start up your computer. A person who can speed up your computer. And about 100,000 other things that we all probably wish we knew how to do ourselves, but don't. The person or people that I know have also done the majority of these things for me for free. This alleviates a lot of phone calls to whoever sold you your computer, and also can save you a lot of money on computer repair people coming to your house. I doubt I am being too clear in this section but I think we all know what I am talking about. Computers can be your best friend in the world, and they can also be the most frustrating. I still have days (but not as many as before) where I want nothing more than to simply throw mine out the window. You need to find yourself someone who knows something about computers and get to know them. It is an invaluable person to have in your life.

The surprise ending to it all.

Here we are, basically, at the end. I hope you found what you read to be useful, I hope you implement it into your daily life, and I am quite confident that it will work for you. The biggest reason why I say this with such confidence is simple—it

worked for me. I don't know of many people who were further in debt than I was, and I also don't know of many people
who have come as far as I have come in the world of personal
finance.

I went through the mindset changes, I sacrificed what I
had to, and I did it. Was there some hard work along the way?
Absolutely. Sacrifice? Without a doubt. But looking back on it
all, there was less hard work and sacrifice than I originally imagined. Also, looking back on it now, it is one of the things that I
am most proud of in my life. I would imagine that most people
who are in debt as much as I was probably stay that way all of
their lives. So I do consider it quite an accomplishment and it
is something that I am very proud of. But, now, I also want to
let you know about somewhat of a surprise ending. When I
say that this is a surprise ending, what I mean is that it became
an unintended consequence of this whole financial journey of
mine. It was never in my plans, it just kind of happened.

If you have not started any of the things outlined in the
book yet, I guess you can disregard this, or maybe you can look
forward to it. Actually, most of you will probably say that I am
crazy and that it will never happen to you.

What I am trying to tell you is this—a lot of things that
I was simply sacrificing in the beginning, things that I told
myself were only for thirty days or six months or whatever—
guess what?? About ninety-nine percent of them became habits
in my daily life.

I told you that I was going to stop drinking Coke for thirty days to save money. Or at least stop buying it from the

convenience store. Well, guess what? Eventually, I stopped buying it from the grocery store, and eventually I stopped drinking it altogether. I have not had a carbonated drink in probably ten years. Not only has it saved me a ton of money over the years, even better, the added benefit is that it is much healthier for me!

I think I already explained about my AC situation. I can easily remember the days when I put it at seventy degrees in the summer time and seventy-eight in the winter. Guess what? After my one summer of seventy-two, then seventy-four, and finally seventy-six, this setting became a habit for me. And the same thing happened with my heat in the winter. I now put it at seventy-six in the summer and seventy-two in the winter, and you know what? I do not feel any colder in the winter or any warmer in the summer.

Another little thing I decided to do during my financial journey was to gravitate a little more towards fresh foods rather than frozen, processed ones. I stopped buying frozen dinners; I started cooking a lot more on my own. Guess what? My freezer is basically empty. Besides chicken or fish that I have stocked up on, there is basically nothing in there. I do just about everything fresh now. Once again, I have saved a ton of money doing this over the years, and again, another added benefit is that it is much much healthier.

So, there you have it, the surprise ending. In the beginning, tell yourself it's just for thirty days. If you're still OK (and alive!) after the thirty days, try making it a few months. I doubt you'll still miss whatever it is you've sacrificed after this amount of time, and you've already reaped the financial benefit.

But you'll probably find that a lot of these things will become habitual in your life, which will make for a lifetime of savings, and also in a lot of cases, a healthier you!

Thank you for your time and thank you for reading my words. I hope you will at least try them, and I hope at least something in this book will help you improve your personal economy. I can assure you without a doubt it should lead to less stress in your life, more happiness, and more opportunities to do the things you really want to do in life.

Stay tuned—I'll have more good stuff to come.

—Dave

AFTERWORD

If you are interested in learning even more about ways to save more, spend less and generate extra cash in your life, visit me at www.yourfinances101.com/blog

There you will find even more tips on the topics discussed in this book and a variety of other ones

Resources

www.yourfinances101.com/blog (my website)

www.bookbyte.com (textbooks)

www.bluerectangle.com (textbooks)

www.annualcreditreport.com (free credit report)

www.creditkarma.com (free credit score)

www.fatwallet.com (various savings ideas)

www.dreamfollowers.com (new business venture)

www.ingramcontent.com/pod-product-compliance
Lightning Source LLC
Chambersburg PA
CBHW071418170526
45165CB00001B/320